EARLY 17th CENTURY MISSIONS of the SOUTHWEST

Frontispiece. *Gran Quivira National monument's two 17th-century churches and the ruins of Humanas Pueblo. Some kivas and house blocks are excavated; unexcavated house blocks can also be seen.*

Photo by National Park Service

EARLY 17th CENTURY MISSIONS of the SOUTHWEST

By FRANCIS B. PARSONS

with Historical Introduction

Book design and drawings by Harold A. Wolfinbarger, Jr.

DALE STUART KING, PUBLISHER
2002 N. TUCSON BLVD., TUCSON, ARIZ. 85716

International Standard Book Number 0-912762-20-9 (paperback)
International Standard Book Number 0-912762-21-7 (clothbound)
Library of Congress Catalog Card Number: 74-32368
Copyright 1975 by Dale Stuart King. All rights reserved.
Manufactured in the United States of America.

ACKNOWLEDGMENTS

For the fine photographs furnished by the
Department of Development, State of New
Mexico, for those from the files of the Museum
of New Mexico, and for the encouragement
of Dr. Bertha P. Dutton of Santa Fé I wish
to express my profound thanks. I wish also to
congratulate Harold A. Wolfinbarger, Jr., for
his fine designs and drawings.

FRANCIS BENJAMIN PARSONS
Silver City, New Mexico
March 2, 1966

Contents

Illustrations

Preface

Back in the 1960's the author, the illustrator, and the editor blithely started preparation of this guidebook and carried it to the typesetting stage.

But various troubles delayed it, and the project became comatose with the death of the author and loss by a printer of much of the illustrative material.

Existence of the worthwhile text and Mr. Wolfinbarger's superb design and illustrations kept nagging me: when my friend Woody Shryock expressed interest in producing the book with his excellent printing facilities (since no similar guide had appeared in the meantime) I was only too glad to obtain replacement photographs to accompany this up-dated manuscript by the late Francis B. Parsons.

The reader should note that this modest guidebook does not pretend to adhere rigidly to its title. San Miguel Chapel and at least one of the El Paso churches were parish churches and not missions; what you see at Pecos and Zuñi, for example, are later structures superimposed on 17th-century remnants; and some existing 17th-century ruins, because they are difficult of access, are omitted, notably in the Galisteo Basin, near Zuñi, and in the Hopi country.

Dale Stuart King
Editor and Publisher
January 5, 1975

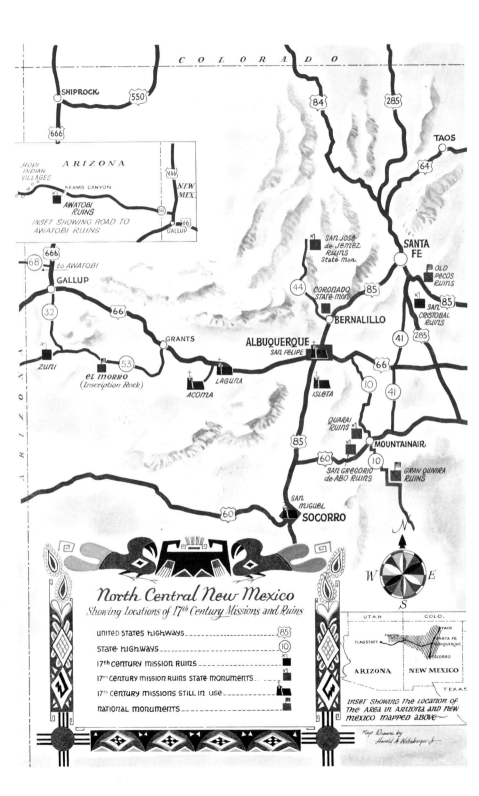

North Central New Mexico

Showing Locations of 17th Century Missions and Ruins

united states highways	85
state highways	10
17th century mission ruins	■
17th century mission ruins state monuments	
17th century missions still in use	
national monuments	

INSET SHOWING THE LOCATION OF THE AREA IN ARIZONA AND NEW MEXICO MAPPED ABOVE—

Map Drawn by
Harold A. Woltenberger Jr.

FOREWORD

 n north central New Mexico along the Rio Grande and its many tributaries, for long centuries before the coming of the white man, vigorous tribes of sedentary Indians lived, built their homes, and cultivated the rich soil bordering the flowing waters. Other such Indians made their homes at the foot of lofty mountain ranges that border the great river; while still others sought favorable locations at the edge of the vast grassland plains to the east. Far to the west, across the mesa lands, people of the Acoma, Zuñi, and Hopi villages, these last in Arizona, flourished. All were farming people and lived in comparative harmony with each other — there was enough for all — dwelling in large, many-roomed homes or *pueblos* of stone or *adobe*.

Indian pueblos or villages may consist of scattered detached houses, or of larger structures, built around central *plazuelas* or courts. Sometimes the larger block houses were several stories high with receding terraced rooms such as may be seen today at Taos pueblo. Square or circular chambers called *kivas* were in the pueblo, and in them the leaders of the community planned the many rites so necessary for the well-being of the group, and performed rain ceremonies and curing rites. The harvest was all important: the Gods of Nature that controlled the seasons, the Gods of Sun and Rain that ensure growth and fertility, must each be propitiated by sacred ceremonies and dances, if corn, beans, squash and other crops were to mature and the pueblo prosper.

It was these peoples, scattered over upland plain and along river valleys, that in the early 17th century under the guidance of Spanish missionaries were to erect large and magnificent churches and *conventos*.

In describing early 17th century Franciscan missions of the Southwest we write of those founded in that area of the northern colony of New Spain known as New Mexico. This vast country claimed by Spain embraced all of the area south of the Arkansas River and westward to the Pacific Ocean. Mission development in the early 17th century was limited to present-day New Mexico, northeastern Arizona and the settlement at Paso del Norte. The later explorations by the Jesuit priest Eusebio Francisco Kino, beginning in the late 1600's in Pimeria Alta, which included southern Arizona, are not included in this book.

As we look today at the sturdy old churches, monuments of stone or adobe, some in ruins, others still serving pueblo or *villa,* we realize that here is a fascinating story, adventurous, romantic, and picturesque, wrought by the industry of inspired Indian and devoted missionaries of the Franciscan order, some 350 years ago.

To understand how and why these massive buildings were reared, we must review a little of the early history of the area, a period beginning with the coming of the Spanish *conquistadores* under the leadership of Francisco Vázquez de Coronado in the 16th century.

HISTORICAL INTRODUCTION

t was early in A.D. 1539, the expedition under the command of Francisco Vázquez de Coronado from Mexico to the unknown north being assured, that a Franciscan monk, Fray Marcos de Niza by name, accompanied by a negro or Moorish slave, Estéban, and a number of native Mexicans, was dispatched to explore the land ahead. Marcos was to bring back to Coronado and his sponsor, Viceroy Don Antonio de Mendoza, full reports of the kind of land encountered, the villages and people he saw, and of course, any and all indications of gold or other treasure. He was also to try and spread the story of the Christian God to the inhabitants and tell of the great white father (the King of Spain) across the wide seas who was to rule over them.

We shall not tell the many details of Marcos' journey here, for it is a long story; nor shall we report on the slaying of Estéban by the Zuñis: suffice it to say the report of the friar to Mendoza and Coronado was so optimistic, his tales of fab-

ulous cities of high buildings covered with gold and turquoise, as glimpsed from a distance, so vivid, that Coronado and his men could hardly await their marching orders. It was thus the so-called "Seven Cities of Cibola" became firmly fastened in the minds of the Spaniards, for all were familiar with the tales of rich booty wrested from the Aztecs and Incas a few short years before.

One year later, in 1540, Coronado and his adventurers, conquistadors all, started north. Entering what is now Arizona, they followed down the San Pedro River to a point near its junction with the Gila. Toiling over desert and rough mountainous country — the *despoblado* (unpopulated zone) — they eventually reached high and well-watered forests in the White Mountains, now a part of an Apache Reservation. Crossing the upper reaches of the Little Colorado River the expedition then turned east along its tributary arroyo of the Zuñi River which led to the first of the sought-for cities. Supplies were running low when the trail-worn Spaniards finally came in sight of Hawikuh, most westerly of the Zuñi pueblos. Today only mounds of shattered walls, it was here Estéban is thought to have met his fate, and here it was necessary for the Spaniards to use force to obtain food. The Zuñis fought bitterly to protect their homes, but superior arms prevailed, and the pueblo was taken over. In this skirmish Coronado, a target in his suit of gilded armor, was injured by flying rocks.

Later, while recuperating in the pueblo, the commander sent out a number of small parties to explore the country and search for other and richer pueblos, for great was their dis-

appointment in finding no treasure in Zuñi. One party, under Captain Hernando de Alvarado, was to go east entrusted with a mission to locate favorable winter quarters for the expedition. It was rumored a number of large Indian villages rich in supplies were located in the valley of a great river there. Alvarado's report was favorable and the Spaniards soon moved into the valley of the Rio Grande, commandeered a large pueblo, forced the people out, and appropriated both their homes and winter stores of food and clothing.

After two long, cold winters and much effort, Coronado and his men, discouraged and disillusioned in their search to find treasure, even to the extent of pursuing a hint of gold into the great plains country far to the northeast, returned in 1542 to distant Mexico.

Two Franciscan friars who were with the expedition elected to remain in the new land. Earnest missionaries, they were convinced that some of the Indians would respond to their teachings. One, Friar Juan de Padilla, returned to the eastern plains where he was greeted by friendly Indians. In his wanderings, ever seeking others to convert, he met a martyr's death at the hands of enemy tribes late in 1542.

Friar Luis de Escalona, a gentle man, built a little hut near the great pueblo at Pecos and there lived for some months. A few of the Indians were friendly but the tribal leaders resented his teachings: he is assumed to have perished there in the winter of 1542.

The first Christian mission in present New Mexico was founded by three Franciscans who entered the country with

7

the Rodriguez-Chamuscado exploring expedition in 1581. The little chapel is thought to have been located at or near the pueblo of Puaray not far from the present Coronado State Monument on the Rio Grande. These devoted men were in advance of their time, for true missionary work could safely come only with permanent settlements by the Spanish. Before long the three friars fell victims to the wrath of the Indian leaders.

It is a historical fact that long before the first of the Californian mission chains was founded in 1769, many of the missions in New Mexico had been soundly built, briefly occupied and long abandoned; both churches and pueblos where they were located fell into ruins. Between 1542 and 1680, twelve priests were murdered, and in the great Pueblo Rebellion of 1680 that swept the Spaniards from the land, twenty-one others lost their lives. Such were the difficulties encountered in attempting to supplant old and venerated deities with a strange God. Nevertheless the patient missionaries persisted and in some 200 years more than 48 missions were founded and thousands of converts made.

Coronado State Monument

few minutes ride on New Mexico road 44 north of Bernalillo and branching west from the Rio Grande valley brings into sight the Coronado State Monument, a large adobe ruin situated high on the terrace above the wide stream. One of the many pueblos of the ancient province of Tiguex, Kuaua, as it is called, is thought to have been the place where Coronado and his men spent the harsh winters of 1540-1 and 1541-2.

This considerably reconstructed, many-roomed structure grouped around two large plazas was at one time several stories high and shows even today how compact and well adapted to a farming economy were the large 16th century adobe pueblos of the Rio Grande Indians. When excavated several years ago by the University of New Mexico, Museum of New Mexico, and the School of American Research, many ceremonial kivas were uncovered. These were subterranean rooms, either round or rectangular in form. In some cases the kiva walls were covered with coats of plaster bearing painted murals depicting scenes relating to the native cosmogony. In one of the rectangular kivas some of the original paintings have been duplicated, making an interesting exhibit.

To house collections of pottery and other artifacts found in the many rooms of the old pueblo a small museum was erected and dedicated at the site in 1940, in observance of the Cuarto-centennial of Coronado's *entrada*. In it are a number of specimens and historic material, or their replicas. There are cactus gardens, an amphitheater, and a gift shop, and future plans include an auditorium and nature trails.

It was the high level of Indian culture as evidenced by Kuaua's inhabitants that presented to the Franciscans, in later

years, the opportunity to reach significant numbers of natives in their work of conversion. To conduct this important task properly the founding at each pueblo of a Christian Mission, consisting of a church and convento, or padre's living quarters, was a necessary feature.

First Settlement and Church

In time, as no treasure of gold or great mineral wealth was found in the new land to the north, the Spanish Crown decided that the country should be settled and the native population converted to the Christian faith.

Settlements were to be established in the valley of the great river; Franciscans were to go to the Indian pueblos and push the work of conversion with energy. Devoted followers of Saint Francis of Assisi, these men traced their long career of missionary work to the founding of the Order of Friars Minor in Italy in November A.D. 1223.

In 1595 the contract to open and develop the colony was finally given to Don Juan de Oñate. Oñate was descended from an old Spanish family, one that played a prominent part in the conquest of Mexico, and was related by marriage to both Hernando Cortés and the Aztec king, Montezuma.

Don Juan de Oñate was authorized to take possession of all lands in the name of Spain; to require the submission of the native population; to find a suitable site for a proposed villa; and to foster the task of converting the natives to Christianity. He was to act as captain-general and *adelantado* (governor) of all his conquests, with authority to grant *encomiendas* or land grants to his followers. He was to receive a government subsidy; the colonists, as first settlers, were to be accorded certain privileges and exemptions. With these concessions went the right to draw upon the conquered natives for labor in developing new plantations.

Many irritating delays harassed Oñate in organizing and assembling his expedition, and it was not until February 1598 that all was ready for the great adventure. Under the command of Vincente de Zaldivar, nephew of Oñate, the caravan pushed north, opening a new and more direct trail from Mexico to the Rio Grande. Accompanied by some 400 soldiers, the settlers with their families and servants wound slowly over the broad plains. Household goods, tools, implements, seeds and the multitude of articles required to found the colony were carried in 83 heavy two-wheeled carts drawn by slow-moving oxen. To stock the ungrazed hills and provide for the needs of the people, more than 7000 horses, cattle and sheep were driven overland. It must indeed have been a thrilling sight as the long procession of men and animals toiled over the drifting sands that lie south of the river.

In April the expedition reached the Rio Grande near present-day Juárez, Chihuahua. Here Oñate formally and with much fanfare took possession of all lands north of the river in the name of King Philip of Spain. After reorganizing the caravan for the long journey ahead, and crossing the river at the ford (El Paso del Norte), the leader with 60 picked men hurried north to locate a site for the settlement.

From the vicinity of Socorro north to the pueblo of Taos, a distance of over 200 miles, in the valley of the great river and its tributaries was the largest concentration of Indian pueblos in the north country. Four language groups were represented in the area, with Tewa and Keresan predominating. The Indians were industrious farmers and hunters living in comparative harmony with their neighbors. This fact was well known by the Spaniards from the reports of earlier explorers. In this region Oñate hoped to found his first colony.

By midsummer, dusty and trail-worn, the caravan reached a Tewa pueblo called *Ok'-he* not far from the junction of the

Rio Grande and Chama rivers. Here, a few weeks earlier, Oñate had been received in friendship by the natives. On the arrival of the caravan the Indians willingly vacated a part of their pueblo for the Spaniards. In appreciation of this generous gesture, legends say, Don Juan de Oñate christened the pueblo "San Juan de los Caballeros" (Saint John of the Gentlemen) a name the pueblo bears to this day. However, the historian Villagrá has a different story. In his *Historia de la Nueva Mexico* he writes the name as being "in memory of those noble sons who first raised in these barbarous regions the bloody tree upon which Christ perished for the redemption of mankind."

One important duty of the commander, as set forth in his royal contract, was the assignment of the missionaries to the field where they were to labor to convert the Indians. Twelve Franciscans, three lay-brothers or *donados* (Christian Mexican Indians), with Fray Alonso Martinez in charge, were to be entrusted with this work. All were equipped for the task with portable altars, sacred pictures and vessels, vestments of brilliant colors and other necessary articles. Experience in Mexico had proved the value of such accessories of color and pomp in making the Christian religion attractive to native peoples.

Each Franciscan was assigned to one or more pueblos. There he would learn the language of the tribe and begin teaching the principles of Christianity. This was a tremendous undertaking for men in a strange land, men totally unfamiliar with the customs and ceremonies of the Indians. For some it was an impossible task and several of the missionaries became discouraged and returned to Mexico. Soon others arrived, and, with those that remained, the real work of conversion started, a work that was to bear fruit in coming generations.

Oñate found a site quite near the pueblo on which to establish his settlement. Called San Gabriel after the Archangel Gabriel, the foundations of this little pueblo have been excavated by the University of New Mexico.

Of interest to this story is the finding of the stone foundations of the first real church built in New Mexico. While there is no doubt that a small temporary chapel was erected in 1598, the foundations uncovered probably belong to the church, built about 1603, which the Spaniards used for about 7 years prior to the founding of Santa Fé. As the building also served as a church for the Indians of nearby San Juan, we may rightly assume it to be the first church erected north of present day Mexico.

The last archaeological work on the ruin, carried on during the summer of 1962, exposed rock and adobe foundation stones that supported the walls of the chancel, the right-hand transept and a small part of the nave.

Lack of building stones in the foundation indicated that the walls of the church were probably made with adobe bricks. The roof, supported on long vigas (rafters) that reached from sidewall to sidewall, and which in turn supported smaller beams and cross-sticks, was covered with about one foot of adobe, slightly crowned in the center to shed rain. While the above method of construction is conjectural, it is common to buildings of that period.

How the interior of the church appeared we may never know, but it is gratifying to students of the early mission churches of New Mexico to have the site of the first church definitely located.

San Miguel Chapel,
Santa Fé

In August 1607 Don Juan de Oñate resigned his commission as governor of New Mexico, to be succeeded by Don Pedro de Peralta. Matters in the little colony were at low ebb in the winter of 1609-10 when the new governor arrived at San Gabriél. Missionary work was almost at a standstill, and there was much dissatisfaction with existing conditions on the

Exterior View San Miguel Chapel, Santa Fé, New Mexico

Photo by New Mexico State Tourist Bureau

part of both colonists and Indians. The authorities in Mexico City had decreed that a new capital should be established in a better location to replace San Gabriel by the river.

Thirty miles south of San Gabriel, near a clear and ever-flowing stream, a tributary of the Rio Grande, a level clearing was selected as the site for a new capital. The Spaniards had ambitious plans for the new city, "La Villa Real de la Santa Fé de San Francisco," as it was called, for it was to be the center of civil and military control for the colony. This is the Santa Fé of today, the oldest capital in the United States, in continuous use (except for 12 years in the 17th century) for some 350 years.

A large plaza was laid out. Facing it on the north, on the foundations of an ancient Indian pueblo, the Governor's "Palace" was built. A long, low building (originally 50 feet longer), it had tower rooms at each end. One was for the storage of military supplies; the other was a chapel for the military and civil personnel of the city. For the citizens of Spanish birth there was only a rude chapel of adobe. This was described by Fray Alonso de Benavides in 1625 as "a rude hut" and he proceeded to erect a new church at once.

During the founding of Santa Fé a large number of Tlax-calan Indians, converted natives from Mexico, settled across the little river that divides the city. Servants and attendants of civil and military Spaniards, they had accompanied their masters on the long journey from that distant land. They lived in small one- and two-room adobe dwellings scattered along the banks of the stream.

Devout Catholics, they early wished for a place of worship they could call their own. Aided and encouraged by the priests and their masters, the Indians banded together, erected a small church and dedicated it to San Miguel (Saint Michael). Although historians feel the walls of the present chapel date from the 1640's, some small part of the first simple building may be incorporated within its walls.

During its long life San Miguel suffered much neglect

and damage. In the great Indian Revolt of 1680, rebels, bent on destroying every trace of the Christian religion, set its woodwork on fire. Even the high vigas supporting the roof were ignited, the Indians tying torches to long poles to reach them. Destruction of the supports of the heavy earthen roof caused its collapse, filling the interior with a mass of flaming wood and scorched adobe. For some years wind and rain played havoc with the remaining walls.

After General Don Diego de Vargas completed the reconquest of Santa Fé in 1693, he gave orders to have San Miguel Church rebuilt. It was not until 1710, however, during the time when Don Marques de la Panuela was governor, that the work is assumed to have been finished. Of considerable historic interest in the rebuilding of the church is an inscription on the carrying-beam of the choir gallery. It reads as follows: *"El Sn Marques de la Panuela Hizo esta fabrica el Alferes Real Dn Agn flos Vergara su criado Ano de 1710."* (The Marquis de Panuela. This building was erected by the Royal Ensign, Don Augustine Flores Vergara in 1710.) The date, on the extreme right of the beam, is somewhat obscured by plaster. Such inscriptions testifying to the largess of patrons were not unusual in early churches.

The floor plan of San Miguel, a simple parallelogram, the side walls slightly drawn in to form the chancel, is of a type used in many small chapels. Walls of adobe rise nearly 50 feet to carry the roof-supporting vigas. The roof itself was finished with about one foot of hard-packed adobe slightly crowned in the center to shed rain. The high walls, sturdy and strong, at one time topped with crenelations, gave to the building a fortress-like appearance. It is believed the church was not equipped with a belltower until some years later.

Four windows high in the nave walls — two are now sealed up — were supplemented by a narrow clerestory window at the chancel crossing. The latter was so placed that afternoon light would flood the altar and reredos. One or two rooms to the right of the nave are later additions, and probably served

View of the ceiling at San Miguel Church.
Photo by Laura Gilpin.

as robing room and sacristy for the officiating padre, who may
have lived in the convento of the nearby parish church.

In the early years of the 19th century the old chapel was
again in deplorable condition. By 1830 it became apparent
to church authorities that if the building were to be preserved
repairs were imperative. The roof leaked badly, but some of
the A.D. 1710 vigas and small beams could be re-used and a new
roof installed. Perhaps the crudely carved corbels of today
were inserted under the vigas at this time. A tower, the quaint
three-stage, stepped-back structure shown in old photographs,
may also have been built at this time.

After New Mexico came under the flag of the United States in 1846, lack of interest and perhaps lack of funds made the old church again vulnerable to storm damage. The bell tower was weakened and during a heavy wind and rain storm in 1872, toppled, causing considerable damage to the front of the building.

Throughout New Mexico, late in the 19th century, there came a growing interest in the historical and religious heritage of the old Spanish colony. This was especially true in Santa Fé where several of the pre-United States buildings survived. San Miguel Chapel was still a shambles from the storm, its interior still filled with debris from the fallen tower. Interest was aroused for its restoration and it is to this restoration that we owe the present appearance of the building.

In this restoration the receded front entrance was retained while above and around it a sturdy square tower with a large open belfry was constructed. This tower, reinforced with strong buttresses, gives dignity to the front facade. The fortress-like crenelations were removed from the top of the outer walls; both the exterior and interior were repaired and replastered; a new roof was built over the old vigas.

Archaeological studies in 1955 in the church brought to light a number of interesting features. Several successive floor levels of hard-packed earth were found under the wood floor; numerous burials were also found, a common practice in old churches; tree-ring readings taken from window and door frames indicated the trees were cut about 1710; the date of the faded reredos was correctly ascertained.

The quaintly carved and painted reredos of wood was carefully restored to its original condition, and now graces the wall behind the altar. During restoration the following inscription was uncovered under the old paint: "This altar was erected through the generosity of Senor Don José Antonio Ortíz, Royal ensign in the year 1798." Six oil paintings fill panels in the upper section of the reredos, some are probably of Mexican origin, others may be the work of native artists. All the paintings have been cleaned and restored to their original brilliancy. Just above the altar table, in a carved and painted niche, is a figure of San Miguel, patron saint of the chapel. San Miguel is flanked by *bultos* of other saints. The whole reredos, so carefully restored, its members repainted and re-gilded, is a fine example of Spanish-Mexican ecclesiastical art of the period.

Historic San José bell, which crashed to the floor when the tower fell in 1872, now rests in an adjoining room, its mellow tone muted to the tap of the visiting tourist. The bell came from Spain and a fascinating story is told of its origin. In 1356 or so, the people of San José in southern Spain, hoping to expel the Moors from their country, made a vow to Saint Joseph that if victory rewarded their efforts they would cast a great bell in his honor. After victory, the vow was fulfilled. Inscribed on the lip of the bell is "SAN JOSE ROGAD POR NOSOTROS. AGOSTO 9 DE 1356." For many years its sweet mellow tone, attributed to gifts of gold and silver cast into the flux, delighted the people of Santa Fé.

What scenes have passed the doors of the old church! Devout Indians, rebel Indians, and generations of earnest people worshipping in the quiet nave. Down from the eastern mesas wound the dusty Santa Fé Trail past the old chapel. Many times, in later years, the village street quiet was shattered by the noise of creaking caravans as they neared the end of the long trek, heading for the longed-for rendezvous in the plaza before the old Governor's Palace.

San Miguel is the chapel of adjacent St. Michael's School. Each day there is a Mass for the school from which the public is excluded. At other times the historic old building is open to the public. Visitors are welcome and a well-informed guide will explain the many unique features to be seen. A visit to the small museum attached to the chapel will be rewarding.

THE 17th
CENTURY MISSIONS

PECOS
National Monument

erhaps the most storied of mission ruins in New Mexico is the old Franciscan church at Pecos, Nuestra Señora de los Ángeles de Pecos. Situated about 30 miles east of Santa Fé, its massive brown adobe walls, a landmark for centuries, crown the south end of a small sandstone mesa not far from the old Santa Fé Trail. Near it sprawls the ruined pueblo of the Pecos people. In A.D. 1540 this was the largest and finest of all the Indian pueblos encountered by the Spaniards. Pedro de Castañeda, foremost of the chroniclers of the Coronado expedition, described it:

"Cicuye (Pecos) is a pueblo containing about 500 warriors. It is feared throughout that land. It is a square, perched on a rock in the center of a vast patio or plaza, with its *estufas* [kivas]. The houses are all alike, four stories high. One can walk on the roofs over the whole pueblo, there being no streets to prevent this. The second terrace is all surrounded with lanes which enable one to circle the whole pueblo. These lanes are like balconies which project out, and under which one can find shelter. The houses have no doors on the ground floor. The inhabitants use movable ladders to climb to the corridors, which are on the inner side of the pueblos. They enter them that way, as the doors of the houses open into the corridors on this terrace. The corridors are used as streets. The houses facing the open country are back to back with those on the patio, and in time of war they are entered through the interior ones. The pueblo is surrounded by a low wall...."

Of these fine Indian homes nothing remains but lofty mounds of scattered stone, a few excavated chambers and a cleared patio. Estimated to have contained several hundred

The brown adobe ruins of the great mission church of Pecos slumber in the bright New Mexico sunlight.

23

rooms, the pueblo's total population in Coronado's time may well have been over 2,000 souls.

The area was first settled about A.D. 1200, the Indians then living in numerous small villages on the banks of the nearby Pecos River. Later — perhaps for purposes of defense — the people joined together and built their redstone pueblos on the high ledges. Easternmost of the great Indian pueblos, its location was ideal for trading with wandering tribes of buffalo hunters. Groups of Indians from the Rio Grande Valley also would gather there each year to exchange shell work, weaving, and other products for bison hides, dried meat, antelope skins, etc.

After the return of Coronado to Mexico in the spring of 1542, two of his Franciscans decided to remain in the country and work with the Indians. Friar Luis de Escalona returned to Pecos but was murdered late in the same year.

Shortly after the arrival of Don Juan Oñate in 1598 missionaries were assigned to Pecos. It was several years, however, before a chapel was built at the pueblo, perhaps as late as 1621. This first of the four churches of Pecos was small and may never have been completed. It was located ¼-mile northeast of the pueblo on a ridge too narrow to accommodate the necessary convento and other secular buildings. Archaeologists from the Museum of New Mexico identified and excavated the structure in 1956.

Fray Andrés Suárez, with grander plans, arrived in 1622 and built "a magnificent temple adorned with six towers, three on each side" (actually the largest European structure in its time north of the present Mexican border). This must have been an impressive landmark for a half century, but was burned in the 1680 Rebellion.

The third church was actually a temporary chapel, prepared after the Reconquest by utilizing the south wall of ruined No. 2 and a massive, parallel convento wall. Its existence was determined by documentary research.

The fourth church, the imposing ruins of which you see

now, was not begun until 1706 but was long thought to be the large 17th-century edifice. It was not until June, 1967 that the late Jean Pinkley, National Park Service archaeologist, encountered massive foundations at a level below the standing walls and realized she had found an older and much larger church.

Mission churches in the Southwest do not conform in type or plan to those the Fathers were accustomed to in Europe. The true cruciform plan with deep transepts had to be modified in favor of a building with a long, narrow nave capable of being spanned with a single heavy timber. This resulted in a building simple in design, in construction, and strictly functional in its arrangement. Transepts were short; walls, adobe or stone, had to be carried up in great thickness, for they must be strong enough to support a roof formed of heavy beams or vigas, these to be crossed by smaller logs or *savinas*, all to be finally covered with a thick coating of adobe. Probably this factor, the problem of spanning a nave without internal support, led the missionaries to pattern their churches on the pueblo construction methods of the Indians.

A few high windows in the nave walls and one over the

John Mix Stanley's sketch of the Pecos church, 1846.

Print courtesy of Museum of New Mexico.

Part of the ruined bell tower of the mission church at deserted Pecos Indian Pueblo.

main door to light the choir gallery, with a clerestory window at the transept crossing, provided ample daylight to the interior.

With the aid of a few hand tools, two or three hand-wrought latches for the doors, and a small supply of nails and metal, all brought from Mexico, these lofty buildings were reared. All other materials were of native origin, the huge vigas being cut in nearby forests and hewn and carved on the site.

Standing in the chancel end of the ruined church, where the old adobe walls are highest, we can trace the long nave by mounds of shapeless bricks that once formed its walls. Under our feet, we are told, rest the bones of two of the early missionaries, found and reburied by Dr. A. V. Kidder of the

Peabody Museum, Harvard University, when excavating in the ruin in the 1920's.

In the distance a high green line of a mesa top cuts across the horizon. In historic times this was a welcome sight to dusty caravans from faraway cities across the vast plains, for at its foot wound the last few miles of the old Santa Fé trail as it led to the Royal City of the Holy Faith of Saint Francis, Santa Fé.

Pecos still had 1,000 people in 1700, but attacks by Comanches increased. In 1746 or 1747 nearly the whole pueblo went out on the plains to hunt buffalo but Comanches ambushed them and killed many people. From this time on, the population declined in size due to continued Comanche harassment as well as smallpox epidemics, until there were only 269 left in 1776. In 1838 the last 17 survivors of the once-thriving town abandoned their ancestral home and joined with their kinsmen at Jémez pueblo.

In August 1846 the old mission was visited and described by Lt. Col. W. H. Emory, a member of the advance guard of the Army of the West, as it moved from Las Vegas to take over the capital at Santa Fé from the Mexicans. A sketch made at that time indicates that much of the old church was standing, as well as a number of the two-story rooms of the convento.

Not long after the conquest of New Mexico by General Kearny's army, settlers began to filter into the area from the "States." They found the massive ruins an easy place from which to secure fine timbers; this resulted in the rapid deterioration of the adobe walls.

In 1965 it was proclaimed a National Monument, to be administered by the National Park Service. A ruins interpretive walk with trailside signs leads to the convento, mission church, remains of the two pueblos, a restored kiva, and other points of interest.

SAN CRISTOBAL MISSION RUIN

ine miles southeast of Santa Fé, on Highway 85, Route 285 leads off to the south, bisecting a broad and lovely expanse of rolling grassland plains, the Galisteo Basin. It was through this country of easy access, long years ago, that Coronado's men traveled on their first visit to the Pecos people. The Basin was the home of the Tano Indians who lived in large villages near springs and small streams that are still to be found scattered over the fertile plains. The Spaniards on first crossing the area reported sighting nine large pueblos, of which five were occupied.

In 1598 Oñate appointed a Franciscan, one Fray Juan de

Rosas, to direct missionary work among the Tano people. However, little or no progress was made in the work of conversion at that time, as mission workers were few, and the good Father was fully occupied in the Rio Grande pueblos which had also been assigned to his care. It was not until 1612 that the task of Christianizing the Tano people really started with the founding of two or three simple missions in the area.

At Galisteo pueblo, above the deep arroyo of the river of that name, a church, Santa Cruz de Galisteo, and small convento were erected. It was once a large pueblo, but today, of these homes and mission buildings, only scattered mounds of rubble dot the plain.

Here in former days a large and prosperous pueblo was situated on the banks of Arroyo San Cristóbal, a short distance below the spot where the stream of clear water emerges from a rocky canyon. Lining both sides of the box-like channel that confines the stream were a number of compact, many-celled homes of the Indians, their exact location now indicated by rounded mounds, depressions, or small fragments of room walls projecting above the drifting sands.

The stream in leaving the pueblo confines flows deep in a red soil cut to drop a few hundred yards away in a graceful curve over a 20-foot crescent cliff into a clear pool. Framed by the green of dwarf willow and lush reeds, it is a delightful spot. How the children of the pueblo in olden times must have enjoyed the clear cool water as they splashed and played in the spray of the little waterfall! Leaving the pool, the streamlet wanders over the grassy plain, skirting deserted pueblos on its course to join the distant Rio Grande.

The large mounded ruins that were pueblo unit houses are situated on both sides of the stream. San Cristóbal was partially excavated in 1912 by Archaeologist N. C. Nelson for the American Museum of Natural History in New York. The pueblo, spread over a large area, was found to consist of several long unit houses of one and two stories in height, with perhaps a total of between 1600 and 1700 rooms. These were arranged around courts or plazas.

A few hundred yards from the main pueblo buildings the Franciscans erected a small chapel and convento. Estimated to have been built around 1630, the mission was a *visita* of nearby Galisteo Mission.

Of the mission itself only a small part of the chancel of the church remains erect. Constructed with thin slabs of sandstone, the well-laid walls rise some 25 feet above the ground with several additional feet buried beneath the debris. For the survival of this small remnant we have to thank the skill of the masons whose clever joining of the angled walls served to brace the structure. The church, originally 70 feet long and 30 feet wide, with walls 3 feet thick, was fronted by a small cemetery *(Campo Santo)*. To the south may be traced low ridges of stone and adobe that were the padre's rooms, the servants' quarters and the corrals. Nelson claims the convento to have had 20 rooms in all.

Eastern portion of ground plan of ruins of San Cristobal pueblo and the small church, built about 1630 and abandoned in 1680.

Plan from N. C. Nelson Galisteo Basin report of 1914

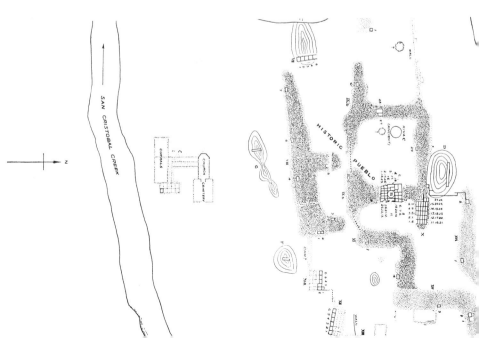

All of the Tano Indians joined in the Great Revolt of 1680. After killing their priests and raiding the missions, the people moved into nearby Santa Fé, occupying the homes and the public buildings of the departed Spaniards. It was not until the reconquest of the province by Don Diego de Vargas in 1692 that they were expelled from the city. The Tano people then joined with other pueblos along the Rio Grande, leaving their former homes to fall into decay.

On a small hill about 150 feet high and situated a little southwest of the pueblo are the remains of a small stone structure. It consists of two circular concentric walls, the outer being about 34 feet in diameter, with sufficient fallen stones to indicate original height too have been much greater. This may have been a watch tower. The inner wall may well have been that of a small hut where watchers would spend the night. The hill provided an excellent lookout for approaching enemies ever eager to raid the more prosperous pueblos.

North of the pueblo a long row of sandstone cliffs contains hundreds of petroglyphs, many of them as fresh looking as when worked by the Indians long ago. Pictured are bird, animal, reptile, and crudely depicted dancing figures intermingled with sacred symbols and other designs.

San Cristobal ruin is on private property, but for those really interested in viewing the ancient mission walls, permission may perhaps be obtained at the nearby ranch house. The restriction of promiscuous tramping over the site is a necessary precaution, for much of the present condition of the church ruin is due to the depredations of pot- and treasure-hunters who in their zeal for non-existing treasure have undermined much of the ancient structure.

MISSION SAN JOSÉ DE JÉMEZ
State Monument

 oming to Bernalillo, N.M., on U.S. 85, you must turn west on State 44 to visit the impressive ruins of the great stone church, San José de Jémez, now the Jemez State Monument. It is an interesting drive, first over miles of semi-desert with distant glimpses of ancient Indian pueblos. Santa Ana pueblo, sheltered by cliffs, is seen just across the Jemez River, then a few miles farther, Zia on its rocky hill looms up, both on sites occupied long before the coming of the white men. At the little farming town of San Ysidro the road turns right and follows up the deep and colorful San Diego canyon alongside a swift mountain stream.

This is harsh country. Steep banded walls of vividly colored sandstone rise layer upon layer to high mesas that confine the Jemez creek to a narrow fertile valley. Framing the sky in the distance are dark, rugged peaks of the Jemez range — a mountain region of high meadows surrounded by dense forests of spruce and aspen where in summer sheep and cattle graze upon the lush grasses. A large pueblo, home of the Jemez Indians, and the little town of Jemez Springs, are passed before the massive ruins of Mission San José de Jemez are reached.

Early in the 17th century a flourishing Indian pueblo called Giusewa "place of hot waters" (hot springs are close by) was located here, one of a number of similar villages strung

32 *Mission church San José de los Jémez, constructed in 1626, stands in ruins in the Jémez State Monument near the town of Jémez Springs.*

along the narrow canyon. Between 1617 and 1629 a strongly-built group of stone buildings dominated by a large church was erected at the pueblo by the Franciscan missionaries. It is quite possible this ambitious mission was built to replace a number of smaller chapels at other pueblos down the canyon, because early accounts indicate that a safer home for both padres and neophytes became necessary as the work of conversion progressed in the canyon.

Many of the Jémez people, especially the leaders, did not take kindly to the efforts of the missionaries to convert them to a new religion. Their own sacred ceremonies and customs were, to them, adequate in every way. As a result of the insistence of the priests there was constant friction between them and the pueblo fathers, and numerous and bloody insurrections occurred throughout the early 1600's, during which a number of the missionaries were killed.

Located on a small level area, the delta of a side canyon, San José was built on a grand scale and is today the most important mission ruin in New Mexico west of the Rio Grande. The massive church with fortress-like walls was obviously erected at a place where it could dominate both the pueblo and the long canyon. Backed by a high mesa it was deemed a safe location; in fact, both location and plan of church and convento seem to indicate a constant fear of attack on the part of its inmates.

To emphasize this feeling of fear we find the ruins of a strongly constructed stone tower rising starkly above the north end of the church. At one time many feet higher, it was topped with an octagonal room containing a rude stairway to its roof. Such a tower must primarily have been built to serve as a watcher's post, for from this high perch nearby mesas and the lower canyon could be well scanned for the approach of strangers, or unfriendly Indians from pueblos in the lower canyon.

Construction date of the mission is thought to be around 1626; tree-ring readings show some of the timbers to have

Tourists wander through the ruins of Jemez Mission, destroyed in the Pueblo Rebellion of 1680. Jemez Indian Pueblo is nearby.

Photo by New Mexico State Tourist Bureau

been cut in 1625; the church was probably in use shortly after this time. The church, 111 long and 34 feet wide, with shallow transepts, is in the form of a simple Latin cross and was a noble building indeed. We may note that the chancel floor is some 7 feet above that of the nave. This unusual additional height was necessary because the bedrock upon which the church stands slants sharply upward toward the north. To have removed the large amount of rock required to bring the floor level to the customary 2 or 3 feet above that of the nave would have been enormously difficult with the crude tools of the time. The greater height thus obtained for the altars became a contributing factor in enhancing the impressiveness of the services, aided of course by the rich furnishings of the chancel and colorful robes of the officiating priests. Several fragments of painted plaster, found when the nave was excavated, indicate the interior to have been embellished with colorful wall decorations, probably executed by native artists working under the direction of the padres.

When the great church was finished its walls rose several feet above the flat adobe roof, an arrangement that would provide a breastwork for defenders in case of need. The interior of the long nave was lighted by a row of windows placed high in the east wall and well above the roof of the adjoining convento. In the west wall, against which a number of the terraced pueblo rooms abutted, no openings of any sort can be traced in the thick wall.

In older times, as today, the padres loved the ancient Christian chants and found much pleasure in teaching apt Indian youths to sing. A choir gallery was always a feature of Catholic mission church construction and San José de Jémez was no exception. Located over the great door at the end of the nave and supported by two sturdy posts, it was lighted by a large window centered over the entrance.

It is evident that relations between the missionaries and the people at Giusewa were quite friendly. Erecting so massive a church and convento as San José required an effort in which padre and convert worked together in harmony. Indian men laid up much of the stone walls, cut timbers in nearby forests and hewed them into shape and size. Women mixed adobe for mortar; it was the women too that so finely plastered the finished walls both inside and outside, even as they do in the pueblos of today.

San José de los Jémez was abandoned about 1630 in favor of a new church, San Diego de la Congregación, with which it has been confused by some early historians, at the present site of Jémez Pueblo.

Knowledge of the long and difficult years of persistent strife between missionary and Indians in Canyon San Diego could be very discouraging to Franciscans assigned to Jemez. They were however men of courage and devotion, and, whenever possible, their work continued.

Even after General de Vargas reconquered the province in 1692 the Jemez remained warlike. In 1696 they rose against the neighboring pueblos and Spanish settlers. De Vargas inflicted great punishment on the Indians at this time, killing many of the warriors. After this defeat the Jemez fled to the Navajo and Hopi country, there to remain until 1716 when they returned to the canyon and built the present pueblo.

The upper reaches of Jemez Creek is picturesque country indeed. A short distance above the mission ruin the canyon narrows, its bottom spanned by a natural dam. Over the centuries thermal springs, bubbling through the surface, have built up a hard travertine mass that today reaches the height of some 20 feet. Through this hard mass, rising as the barrier increased, the swift mountain stream has broken a channel, creating a foaming fall of noisy beauty. The setting of the unique dam — the rushing waters have deposited on the weathered mass the multicolored patina of age — and the wild unspoiled beauty of the canyon make the spot an interesting feature of the region.

There is a visitor center at the site and a resident monument ranger.

MISSION SAN GREGORIO DE ABÓ
State Monument

 ear the thickly forested slopes of the blue Manzano Mountains, overlooking the rolling Estancia plains to the east, are to be seen the imposing ruins of two early 17th century Indian Missions, San Gregorio de Abó, and Quarai. This picturesque country, ancient territory of the Piros and Tiguas (Tiwas), was first visited by Spanish explorers in 1583. They found the Indians living in fine stone pueblos placed in sheltered locations, and noted that the country provided everything required for the needs of the inhabitants. Salt was available in the salt lagoons beyond the plains. Bison hides and antelope skins bartered with roving tribes of hunters contributed to the economy, and it was evident the pueblos were thriving, the people strong in their mountain homes.

Six miles west of Mountainair, a little town spanning U.S. Highway 60 some 40 miles east of the Rio Grande, lie the ruins of San Gregorio de Abó Mission. A short spur road, now paved, dips down to cross Arroyo Abó, pulls out and ends at an impressive pile of massed red sandstone that was the old mission buildings. Some degree of stabilization work has been done, beginning in the 1930's, to the ancient structure, thus preserving for us the lines of the great church walls and many of the convento rooms. Both San Gregorio and Quarai are state monuments under the care of the Monuments Division of the Museum of New Mexico.

In locating their missions in relation to existing pueblos

Considerably repaired, the ruins of the church at Abó Pueblo attest the construction ability of the now extinct Piro Indians working under Franciscan friars.

Photo by Hiram L. Parent

the Franciscans had certain objectives in mind essential to the success of their work, objectives that perhaps we can trace to Abó. As we stand on the mounded walls at the far end of the large quadrangle, walls that once were Indian homes, and look over the central plaza before us, we note that both church and convento were constructed close to the pueblo but outside its actual boundary. There were several reasons for this and the first would be lack of space in the pueblo itself, for, as we shall see, the Fathers planned their missions on no mean scale. They envisioned an establishment that would impress the converts with the grandeur of the new religion, and also, in time, would encompass and dominate both the religious and secular life of the people: a community living in complete harmony.

*The red sandstone ruins of the mission church at abandoned Abó
Pueblo ruin lie just off U.S. Highway 70 near Mountainair, N.M.*
Photo by Hiram L. Parent

Mission plans therefore called for a site with ample room
for expansion. To allow for this the church was usually placed
at one side of the pueblo with the great door facing it. The
convento — a large rectangular block of rooms containing
quarters for the priests and servants — was located so as to
connect with the church on the side most removed from the
pueblo. Such an arrangement provided the padres with some
degree of privacy, and perhaps a measure of protection in
case of trouble. Locating the convento in this manner allowed
its roof walks to become vantage points from which the missionaries could keep watch on the daily comings and goings of
the Indians. Time proved — in many missions — that this

arrangement was not adequate for safety, for unwise attempts to dominate the life of these proud people cost many a missionary his own.

The large church, its construction credited to Fray Francisco de Acevedo, was built between 1627 and 1644. Of the fine red Abó sandstone, a colorful and excellent material, its walls were comparatively thin. This type of construction necessitated the placing of massive stone buttresses on the north to reënforce that wall so it could support the heavy roof timbers (vigas). The opposite wall was strengthened by the abutting convento chambers. The vigas at Abó were in groups of four, hewn by hand and strengthened with finely carved corbels set in the wall under each pair. The heavy vigas were then crossed with smaller poles (savinas), probably of the lighter aspen wood. All was then covered with a foot or so of earth. This packed surface — crowned in the center so as to shed water to the projecting rain spouts — when kept in repair, formed an excellent roof.

Looking closely we note the viga recesses in the walls of the chancel to be some 8 feet above those of the nave. This arrangement, common in most early churches, allows ample space above the main roof for a cross clerestory window to span the nave at the transept crossing. It was largely by means of clerestory windows that the priests were able to flood chancels and altars of their churches with brilliant daylight. It may be noted that milleniums ago the ancient priests of the Nile Valley lighted the inner sanctuaries of their great temples by means of clerestory windows.

Quite early the padres trained willing converts to sing and even to play simple musical instruments. Music and group chanting appealed to the Indians and added considerably to the attraction of the new religion. Choirs were soon formed and in each church a choir gallery constructed, usually at the lower end of the nave, as a balcony spanning the space above the great doorway. Lighted by a large window centered over the entrance, the gallery at Abó was supported on two sturdy posts and entered by means of a stone stairway attached to the exterior wall of the building.

Interior walls of mission buildings were finished with a plastered surface, those of the church receiving especial care to serve as a ground for future painted decorations. To smooth out the inequalities of the rough stone walls, several plaster coats were required, the last being composed of sharp sand mixed with a small amount of either kaolin or gypsum to form a smooth hard surface. Painted by native artists under the direction of the padres, composed of home-mixed earthen colors, the results, while crude, were brilliant and effective. Most of the finer work was centered in the chancel and around the altars, the nave probably being finished in plain tints with a dado of banded color or of simulated tiling copied from samples brought from Mexico. Such was probably the treatment of the church at Abó, for a number of painted fragments of plaster were found when the nave was excavated.

Let us use our imagination and try to picture this fine church during its days of full glory. Bathed in the muted light of a brilliant New Mexico day filtering through the clerestory window . . . a gentle breeze flickering the lighted candles on the altars . . . the priests in bright robes intoning the mass and the converts devoutly kneeling . . . one would indeed feel that here the work of the Franciscans had reached fulfillment. Such was not the case, for by 1670 repeated attacks by Apaches and others made life untenable, and both pueblo and mission were abandoned.

In one of the inner courts of the convento is the remains of a round kiva, a ceremonal chamber used by the Indians from time immemorial, a feature we shall see again at Mission Quarai. Note, too, a narrow room with stone birdroosts. Did the padres appreciate the fine qualities of our native turkeys? Feathers were used in many Indian ceremonies, so perhaps it may be that a wise padre allowed his converts to keep birds here and use their feathers in some of the pueblo festivals, thus tempering to some extent the austerity of the new religion.

MISSION QUARAI

winging north from Mountainair on State Road 10 we cross the rolling plains to visit another old Franciscan mission, this one nestled in the foothills close to the forested Manzano Mountains. A deserted homestead or two are passed, each with dilapitated shacks, weathered and gray, melancholy reminders of the struggles of early settlers. One cannot help but wonder if the ways of the pueblo people, as developed by years of living in this land of little rain, were not better adapted to a successful existence here.

It is, however, a country of park-like hills, sparsely covered with pinyon and juniper, all reaching back to the beautiful green forest of the mountain slopes. Eastward the vast Estancia plains flatten out to a thin line beyond which lie the distant salt lakes.

Turning left at the little native village of Punta de Agua we glimpse through the trees old red stone walls standing high and solitary: the ruined church at Quarai.

It is thought that Friar Estévan de Perea, sponsor of many of the early 17th century missions in New Mexico, established Quarai in 1630, and dedicated the mission, calling it the Church of the Immaculate Conception. An early chapel foundation has recently been uncovered in the main plaza. A plain rectangle, it measured approximately 50 by 19 feet, inside dimensions. The walls averaged 30 inches thick and the building was constructed with sandstone slabs.

This small building, unknown until brought to light in

Distant view of the massive ruins of Quarai Mission in the deserted pueblo of the same name.

Photo by New Mexico State Tourist Bureau

1959, was probably the first Christian building at Quarai. The large church and extensive convento, which came later, are believed to be the work of Fray Francisco de Acevedo.

As at Mission Abó, the active life of Quarai was short. After flourishing for some years, it had by 1650, in common with others in this isolated region, reached its peak of activity. Twenty years later both Indian homes and mission buildings were abandoned, never again to be reoccupied.

Let us try to reconstruct the story of the growth and development of this fine Indian pueblo, a pueblo with a long pre-Spanish history.

In olden times, under ancient trees, hunters found fine springs of clear, cold water fed by melting snows from the high peaks. The little glen early became a favorite camping place. Game was plentiful — the forests abounding with deer and elk—while on the plains the fleet antelope could be stalked or driven into huge traps. Through the long years there was a slow change in the habits of the people from a strictly hunting and food gathering economy to one in which agriculture played a large part; later Indians of the Tigua tribe settled near the springs. At first simple shelters were erected, but as more dependence on the harvest prevailed, the natives found that better protection was necessary if the cold, harsh winters were to be passed in comfort. Large and well-built homes of stone gradually replaced the early brush and mud-plastered shelters; crops were good and the pueblo thrived. When missionary work first commenced at Quarai, well over 600 people were living in two large terraced stone buildings.

We see today, of pueblo and mission, only the ruined walls of the great church looming high upon the scene. Strongly built of the red Abó sandstone, 4 to 6 feet thick, they reach in places almost to their original height and are indeed an impressive reminder of the skill and energy of the builders.

As we stand in the large doorway of the church and look toward the chancel we become increasingly aware of the vast size of the massive building. Measuring 104 feet by 50 feet, the true straight walls still so inclose the interior that an illusion of the perfection of the finished building is apparent. Flat slabs of stone pave the floor, an unusual feature in early churches where hard-packed adobe was the customary finish.

Walking the length of the nave and looking back we see through the great doorway and choir window above the green of large cottonwoods clustered about the old mission well. Two sturdy bell towers, one at each corner, once graced the front of the edifice, lending both dignity and balance to its design. Viga sockets piercing the front wall are an indication that the supporting beams of the choir gallery projected on the exterior and probably carried a narrow balcony over the entrance, an arrangement common in many of the early churches.

Many years ago the noted archaeologist, Adolph Bandelier, found the convento walls at Quarai reduced to foundation

lines. Work undertaken by the Museum of New Mexico in recent years (Quarai is a state monument) has resulted in a partial rebuilding and stabilizing of the walls.

In each of the two convento courts is a kiva ruin; one is square, the other round like that at Abó. Why did the padres allow these copies of pagan ceremonial chambers to be incorporated into their missions, especially so near their living quarters? Could it be they thought conversion might be made easier if by gradual means some of the ancient Indian ceremonies could be welded into the new religion? Many of the indigenous ceremonies were of a social nature, and certainly the Christian religion must not be made to appear too strange to the neophytes. Even today in many of the pueblo ceremonies the two are blended together with first a church service, followed by the Indian dances and other activities. Kivas, too, are used as clubhouses in which the younger men of the tribe are instructed in ceremonial lore. Perhaps at Quarai they were so used under the watchful eyes of the padres.

In the few years before its abandonment the Apache menace at Quarai was strong. They controlled the trail to the salt lakes, made frequent raids on the pueblo and made living increasingly difficult. Fear of future attacks was strong, but it would seem that the final abandonment of the mission was peaceful, the people leaving to find a greater measure of security. For a time they joined the Indians at nearby Tajique, finally in 1680 or so retreating with the Spaniards to Paso del Norte (Juárez, Chih.).

Franciscan Quarai is incomparable in its lovely setting. Here the visitor, be he historian, archaeologist, nature-lover or artist, will find a rewarding wealth of interest and pleasure as he wanders at will through the ancient ruin and enjoys the unspoiled beauty of hill and mountain forest.

The monument is protected by resident personnel, and there is a fine museum.

Apache Indians drove the peaceful residents of
Quarai from their pueblo in A.D. *1674, and the*
church fell into ruin.

MISSION OF THE HUMANAS
Gran Quivira National Monument

wenty-five miles south of Mountainair, located in a reservation known as the Gran Quivira National Monument, are perhaps the best outlying early Franciscan frontier mission ruins in New Mexico. A paved highway (Route 14) winds over the wide plain and along the eastern edge of the Chupadera Mesa with only a few ranch houses dotting the interminable expanse of range land. It is a land of far horizons and distant blue mountains, a lonely and lovely region cupped in the inverted bowl of a brilliant turquoise sky.

At length, in the distance, a rugged rock-crowned hill is seen rising abruptly from the plain. Upon this eminence in in ancient days Indians of the Piro tribe built their homes, farming the fertile acres of the plain below. Within the confines of the 611-acre national monument are the fallen walls of some 21 stone pueblos, and the ruins of two mission churches.

It was late in the 16th century, 1581 - 83 to be exact, when the Rodriguez-Chamuscado expedition first marched into this country. Twenty years later, after the first settlements in the Rio Grande Valley were well established, more missionaries

Looking out through the entrance of San Buenaventura mission church at Gran Quivira National Monument, N.M.

Photo by New Mexico State Tourist Bureau

arrived from Mexico. A number of these earnest monks were assigned to the more distant pueblos, hitherto neglected because of lack of workers, and the task of converting the natives was under way.

Fray Alonso de Benavides, appointed *custodio* of the missions in the new colony, visited this area in 1628 or 1629. His report to his superiors in Mexico states that there were a number of large pueblos scattered throughout the region, inhabited by thrifty farming people, perhaps to the number of 10,000 souls. He noted also that six missions had been founded among them, each with its small chapel, and that the work of conversion was well started. It was Benavides who first called these remote settlements "Villages of the Humanas", but to the Spaniards in later years all the pueblos east of the Manzano Mountains were called the "Saline Pueblos".

The people were good farmers, water was never plentiful, but through years of experience they learned to conserve the meager rainfall. It is thought a system of small earthen dams and storage tanks collected the runoff from the infrequent showers. The water then could be gradually released as needed to the fertile soil, and good crops resulted. Traces of early irrigation systems however have long disappeared. During the Spanish occupancy at the pueblo missions they noted the water supply as coming from some 32 shallow wells a quarter of a league from Gran Quivira. These have long since filled with drifting dust.

The first mission church built by Father Francisco de Letrado, probably in the year 1629, was dedicated to San Isidro. It was a typical early church, consisting of a simple parallelogram composed of a long nave and the chancel. Small recesses were at each side of the altar, probably used as storage closets for the sacred vestments and other articles required in the services. The low stone walls that remain of this early chapel are dwarfed by a high mound of stone to the north, all that remains of a tall, terraced Indian home.

In time it became evident to the Franciscan authorities,

that the numerous small missions in the area, all administered as *visitas* from San Gregorio de Abó, would be better served if a large church and convento were to be erected at the largest of the Humanas villages. The new church must be massive and imposing, and the convento of ample size to house a number of missionaries, lay brothers, their servants, and horses or burros. By stocking the mission with sheep and cattle it was felt the animals would multiply rapidly on the fine native grasses and become an important scource of revenue.

Most Humanas missions reports perished in the Pueblo Rebellion of 1680, although copies might be found some day in Spanish archives. Until then we won't know exact dates for the various construction projects, or the names of the priests connected with them. We do know, however, that Friar Diego de Santander started the large church in 1659. To be called San Buenaventura de las Humanas, it was to crown the highest point on the hill — a church militant, planned to dominate the country for miles around. Massively constructed with the native blue-gray limestone, it was to measure 140 feet in length, a sturdy and enduring monument to Christianity.

Some years ago when the large church was excavated by National Park archaeologists, evidence seemed to indicate that the connected convento was the first project undertaken in the new conception, and to have been occupied early by the missionaries. With the Fathers comfortably housed, the building of the great church could follow at a more leisurely pace, for it undoubtedly was to be a major piece of construction.

Shown on page 53 is the ground plan of the mission. This drawing based on uncovered foundation lines, is the work of engineers of the National Park Service. A little study will show how carefully thought out was the Fathers' conception of their mission as a large and efficient working unit. Comfort, convenience, and privacy is plainly evident in the arrangement of the many apartments; even the porter's lodge which gave access to the convento was placed outside its actual confines. Here on stone benches, petitioners, perhaps with children

The blue-gray walls of the great church crown the limestone mesa at Gran Quivira National Monument.

to baptize, or with other problems, could await the priest's convenience, for they were busy men.

Centered in the convento is a small enclosed patio, its walls broken by large window openings. Surrounded by an ambulatory or roofed-over cloister it was a place where the missionaries could meditate or rest enjoying the quiet of an inner sanctuary. We may be sure the patio in its day had bright flowers and shrubs so dearly loved by the padres: a bit of Old Mexico transplanted to the new home.

The floor of the great church is of the customary cruciform shape, slightly narrowing toward the chancel, and with shallow transepts. The whole concept shows considerable refinement over earlier church plans. The large central doorway facing the pueblo plaza has sharply splayed sides against which the heavy doors of wood were to swing. Early heavy doors of this type had on the jamb or outer stile pivots that, set in

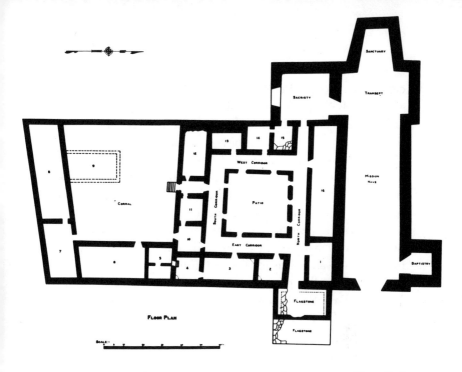

Floor plan of San Buenaventura mission and convento at Gran Qui-vira National Monument, N.M.

Courtesy National Park Service.

sockets, acted as hinges on which the doors would swing.

Conveniently located just inside the nave on the right is a small baptistry with place for font and drain. At the other end of the nave the two transepts are sharply defined, each containing ample room for an altar. Connecting with the south transept was the sacristy or robing room. Here were kept the sacred vessels, missals, and other articles used in the celebration of the Mass. Connected to the convento by two small doors, it led directly into the chancel, giving the necessary privacy to the padres as they passed from their chambers to the church.

The remaining limestone walls that once were part of the large church dwarf all other ruins on the hill. Six feet or more in thickness, they were constructed to carry huge, roof-supporting, hewn vigas. The indefatigible Adolph Bandelier on his visit to Quivira in 1880 writes: "Huge beams, quaintly carved like those at Pecos, but more massive, fairly hewn, and approximately squared, are still in place across the doorways and in some parts of the interior of the church, but the roof is completely gone. Much rubbish fills the interior, and from appearances I should judge that the roof was never finished over the whole church." Some historians today believe the church to have been completed and in use for some years before the abandonment of the pueblo.

It would appear that when settlers first homesteaded the nearby plains many of the beams and most of the other wood in the ruins was "salvaged" for local use. Fortunately a few of the carved smaller beams were located and retrieved by the National Park Service and probably will be returned to the monument for exhibit when adequate museum facilities are constructed.

Stables, sheds and corrals were close at hand, as well as quarters for the servants. From early records we learn that a mission as large as San Buenaventura would have at least 20 servants selected from the faithful. To the women fell the cooking, cleaning, laundry work and perhaps, as they became skilled with the needle, the task of keeping the church linens in repair. The men cared for the animals, worked the padre's land allotment, provided the fuel, and took on the other heavy chores. Boys were trained for the choir with selected ones serving as acolytes.

Recently the foundations of one of the six small missions noted by Fray Alonso de Benavides in 1628–29 as being in this area have been found. Excavations carried at the site of old Tabirá (Pueblo Blanco) some 15 miles northeast of Gran Quivira, by the Museum of New Mexico, resulted in the uncovering of the foundation of white sandstone slabs. Centered in the main plaza of the pueblo, the church was approximately 60 feet long and perhaps 33 feet wide. Careful study of the ruin indicated two periods of construction: the first probably occurred in 1628 or so; the other, a renovating job, may have been done as late as 1659 when San Buenaventura was under construction.

The Saline pueblos — Gran Quivira, Abó, Tabirá and others in this remote country — have long been known as the "Cities That Died From Fear". In those early days it was impossible for the civil authorities in distant Santa Fé, with their small military garrison, to provide adequate protection to the outlying missions. As the missions grew in wealth, as their herds and flocks increased, they became prey to the marauding Apache. When military protection ceased, the converted peoples lacked strength to fight off enemy attacks, and fear assailed them. Crops were raided at will, converts killed or captured and sold into slavery; a long period of drought descended on the land and the people lost heart. With both men and nature against them, Indians and missionaries alike could not hold out and gradually moved from the area. By the late 1670's every village and mission in the vast Saline country was deserted, the people seeking shelter in safer communities along the Rio Grande Valley.

It is sad to contemplate that San Buenaventura, a mission so thoughtfully conceived, so ambitiously planned to be an enduring rock of Christianity to the natives of this wide land, had to be abandoned to the mercy of the elements.

It is a commentary on the fighting skill of the wandering Apache tribes that this country, for well over 200 years, became a desert shunned by all. This condition lasted until the Apache menace was finally ended in the latter part of the 1800's, and homesteaders filtered in.

The National Park Service has long hoped to add Abó and Quarai to Gran Quivira to create a Salinas Missions National Monument.

ISLETA MISSION
and Pueblo

 few miles south of Albuquerque, where the valley of the Rio Grande widens, is situated the pueblo of the Isleta Indians. Southernmost of the homes of the Tiguex (Tee-gwesh) people, its fertile acres span the flowing waters of the great river. A well-established and thriving community long before the coming of the Spaniards in 1580, its fortunate location some 30 leagues below the winter quarters of Coronado's men saved the pueblo from the exploitation experienced by the northern people at the hands of disappointed treasure seekers. In later years the same 30 leagues enabled the Isletans to avoid much of the friction that developed in the upper valley between civil and religious authorities, friction that wore down the nearer pueblos and contributed to the rebellion of 1680.

Franciscans founded the first mission in Isleta in 1613, dedicating it to San Antonio de Padua. It was a crude, adobe structure that served the people well, for the Indians took

San Antonio de Isleta church at Isleta Pueblo near Albuquerque, New Mexico, before it was returned to its appearance of ancient Spanish times.

Photo by New Mexico State Tourist Bureau.

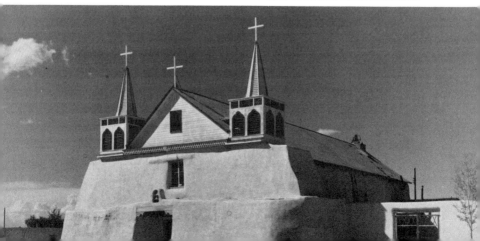

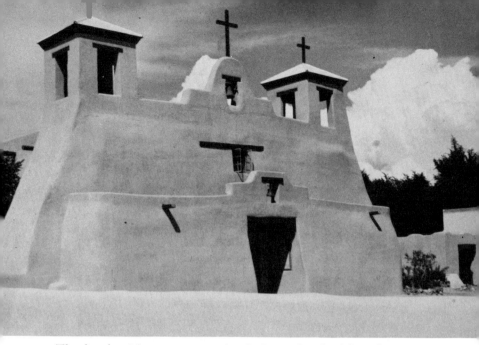

The church at Isleta as it appears after the "gingerbread" of the early 1900's had been remodeled to the old Spanish style again.

Photo by author

kindly to the new religion and many were baptized. It is thought the early mission occupied the site of the present church and that some of its walls were incorporated in this building when it was erected in 1710. It was to Isleta and Socorro pueblos that many of the Piro Indians fled when their homes were abandoned in the 1670's.

We may recall that in 1680, after the successful attack of the rebel Indians on Santa Fé, the retreating Spaniards under Governor Antonio de Otermin gathered at Isleta pueblo. From this pueblo, too, the Governor led the surviving Spaniards and 385 of the converted Indians on the long hard journey to El Paso del Norte. Other Indians (those who remained behind) fled to the hills, or joined nearby pueblos; by 1681 the home of the Isletans was completely abandoned. Rebel Indians then burned the convento and church but the thick adobe walls of the latter resisted the flames and remained standing.

During the reconquest of the province by de Vargas in

1692 Isleta became his first headquarters and from it he launched a number of expeditions which soon reduced the nearer pueblos to submission. Shortly after the re-occupation of the pueblo many of the former inhabitants, those who had sought shelter in the hills, returned to their old homes. The Franciscan friars at once started rebuilding the mission, always a first task with the devout Spaniards. The pueblo homes were made livable and crops again planted as the season permitted.

The present church, containing parts of the walls of the old building, was finished about 1710 under the direction of Fray Juan de la Peña. Dedicated to Saint Augustine, it stands on a slight mound above the ancient Campo Santo and faces the large central plaza of the pueblo.

In its long, continued use — well over 240 years — the old church has undergone many changes. Constructed of large adobe bricks, the rambling walls, quaint and irregular in outline and strongly buttressed had, during the 1800's, slowly weathered into a picturesque texture. To the right of the church, behind crudely shaped arches, were the convento rooms.

When in 1776 Fray Francisco Atanasio Dominguez conducted his tour of inspection of the missions of New Mexico he found the Isleta Mission to be without a priest but the church to be in fair condition. Part of the convento, he noted, was two stories in height and the Padre's allotted garden was in fine condition.

When the pueblo was abandoned in 1680, the mission bells, three in number, were buried under the floor of the church. Dug up after the reconquest, two were rehung in the new belfries; the third was sent to El Paso del Norte. Perhaps it was intended for use in the new Ysleta pueblo founded in 1681 just below El Paso, Texas.

Some years ago the two peculiar box-like bell towers that framed the entrance were sheathed in wood and surmounted with short, sharp spires covered with sheet metal. Louvered openings concealed the bells. At this time also a pitched roof of sheet metal covered the nave. The use of such materials detracted much from the dignity of the ancient building, a dignity that has happily been restored during the recent remodeling of the church.

A new and enlarged porch has been added to the church, the two towers rebuilt, and the large, angled buttresses which slanted down from the roof line strengthened. Above the great door and choir window a simple arched opening contains the mission bell. The walls have been neatly replastered and over all the three traditional crosses stand high.

The above restorations carried on at Saint Augustine's church at Isleta have resulted in a building of uncomplicated beauty, conforming to the age-old traditions of early Franciscan pueblo-mission structures. It is a joy to behold and pleasing to all lovers of the early, functional adobe buildings created by devout padre and Indian convert so many yeras ago.

Entering the interior, one is immediately impressed with the restful treatment of the wall surfaces. One notes, too, the ancient weathered vigas with crude carved corbels of native pine at each end, structural features that support the restored flat roof. In the traditional position facing the chancel is the attractive choir gallery.

The small chancel (the church still retains its original size) is bathed in the bright afternoon sunlight which filters through a narrow clerestory window, a traditional feature of early mission churches. Attention is thus fastened upon the handsome crucifix suspended above the high altar. Inside the communion rail a few old Navajo rugs grace the wooden floor.

At intervals on the nave walls, charmingly executed in blue and white ceramic tiles, are the Stations of the Cross. The simplicity of these panels — a slight tint of green is used in the garments — is in pleasing contrast to the brilliantly colored ones so often found in other churches. We except, of course, the faded oil paintings, work of devout native artists, still found in a few of the older pueblo churches. In Isleta each station is framed with a band of terra-cotta paint that contrasts nicely with the soft buff of the walls.

The interior of the old church even today is one of simplicity; the exterior conforms to the spirit of ancient adobe missions, the overall appearance bears testimony to the affection of the people of Isleta for their parish church. They are a friendly people, are comfortably situated on their well-watered ancestral plantations, and welcome the casual visitor who expresses interest in and appreciation of their ancient mission (now parish) church of Saint Augustine. (Spanish: *San Augustín de Hippo*).

SAN MIGUEL
Mission Church, Socorro

 n the Rio Grande Valley 75 miles south of Albuquerque in the old town of Socorro is San Miguel Mission Church. This ancient building is noteworthy both for its excellent condition and the fact that in the present structure is incorporated a small part of the early church erected between A.D. 1616 and 1628. Built with thick adobe walls, the building is considered to be an excellent example of early Spanish-Indian mission architecture.

In olden times a pueblo of the Piro Indians was located near the present town, perhaps under its very foundations. In documents relating to the Oñate expedition (1598) the pueblo bore the name Piloque. It was in this village, after the long, grinding trip across the arid desert — the 90-mile Jornada del Muerto — that Oñate found friendly Indians who supplied the travelers with needed provisions. A few years later Fran-

San Miguel Church at Socorro, New Mexico.
Photo by Laura Gilpin

ciscan missionaries erected a small chapel at the pueblo, nam-
ing it Virgin del Socorro (Virgin of Relief) to commemorate the
aid given to Oñate, and to other weary caravans that followed.
A small mission, it was to serve the Piros here, and at other
pueblos in the vicinity, including one at San Antonio 11 miles
further south. All signs of these ancient pueblos have long

vanished, as have the people who lived in them. During the early years of the 1600's, as more and more caravans traveled between Mexico and the new colony, Socorro Mission grew in importance.

We have previously told how in the late 1670's terrible times plagued the many Saline pueblos to the east; and how, unable to withstand the raids of enemy Indians, the Piros fled their homes and sought shelter in friendly Socorro. Later, when the Rebellion of 1680 broke over the land, the Piros and people of Socorro remained at peace with the settlers, many of them abandoning their pueblos and joining the Spaniards in the retreat to El Paso del Norte.

In time the refugee Indians from Socorro and the Saline pueblos founded new homes on the fertile banks of the Rio Grande a few miles from El Paso del Norte. These towns have survived to this day.

With the reconquest of New Mexico by de Vargas (1692-93) a few of the Indians returned to their former homes, and shortly afterwards the Franciscans rebuilt the ruined church, dedicating it as Misión Nuestra Señora del Socorro. It is now called San Miguel.

It later became the ambition of the padres at Socorro to make of their church one of the richest and most beautiful in the province, comparable indeed with many in Old Mexico. The exterior design, although somewhat changed in the course of years, is beautifully proportioned. Twin towers rise in three stages, and are roofed with small domes over which rise the crosses. A gothic-like tracery that adorns the towers is undoubtedly a much later addition.

Rich silver mines in the nearby mountains, worked by the devout Indians, produced the metal used to embellish the church interior. Tabernacle, communion rail and the sacred vessels were of solid silver, while gorgeous liners and embroideries decked the altars. When the retreat of A.D. 1680 com-

Another view of San Miguel mission church, Socorro.

Photo by Laura Gilpin

pelled quick abandonment of the mission, all the church treasures were buried by the priests. A map of the exact spot was made by one of the padres, only to be lost in the flight for safety. This rich treasure, so we are told, still lies in some unknown place beneath the shifting sands of New Mexico.

The interior of the old church is impressive in its simplicity. Walls finished white set off the stained glass windows and bring into bold relief the colorful Stations of the Cross. Time-stained vigas that once supported a flat roof now uphold the ceiling. A string-course moulding tops the long nave walls. Crudely carved to represent the cord that ties the course habit of Franciscan monks together, it supports corbels that tie the vigas to the walls. The ancient choir gallery is still in place over the main door and the atmosphere of olden times pervades the building. As it actively serves as a parish church, certain concessions to modern comfort have been made.

Modern Socorro was established as a villa by the Spanish government of Mexico in 1817 when 21 settlers were granted fertile acres along the Rio Grande. By this time we may truly assume that the Indians had long disappeared from the scene or were living in the village of Socorro established south of El Paso del Norte in 1681.

It is interesting to note that oldtime Spanish villas when laid out in the northern colony consisted of land one league in all directions from a central point. The Spanish league was 2.64 miles in length and the land included in the square grant totaled 17,000 acres.

With the rediscovery and reworking of the rich silver mines in the nearby mountains Socorro become a busy trading center. During the latter part of the 1880's it was the third largest city in New Mexico, possessing its full share of saloons, gaming establishments, and other institutions which always spring up where wild and lawless characters gather. Today it is a picturesque Spanish-American community, the county seat, and the home of the New Mexico Institute of Mining and Technology.

REBELLION OF THE PUEBLO INDIANS

lthough the earliest missionary work by the Franciscans among the pueblo Indians in New Mexico dates from the time of the Fray Augustín Rodriguez expedition in 1581, and was followed shortly after by the padres with Oñate in 1598, no buildings of that period, mission or otherwise, are standing today. Shortly after the turn of the 17th century, as the ranks of the gray-robed friars increased, mission work was greatly extended in scope. In 1631 the total number of missionaries listed as working in the province was 66. More and larger missions were founded and many fine churches built. Comparatively few of these early 17th-century buildings have survived to this day, most of them falling before the savage onslaught of attacking Indians at the time of the great Pueblo Rebellion of 1680.

During the time when outlying missions were active, functioning institutions, unrest was developing and growing in intensity within the Rio Grande pueblos. Sporadic revolts broke out as some of the Indians sought to break away from Spanish domination. Exploitation by both religious and civil authorities — the latter in demanding free labor and tribute, the former in a continuous and at times harsh suppression of ancient rites and ceremonies — fostered resentments which finally flamed into the deadly outburst. The unwise and unnecessary oppression by the Spanish people in dealing with the non-conforming Indian, the whipping, imprisoning — even hanging and selling into slavery of those who resisted the authority of State or Church — hastened the debacle.

During the 1660's severe drought plagued the province, food was in short supply, the granaries of the missions were empty and the people suffered. It was natural that some of the pueblo leaders should think the Christian God had deserted them and appeal to their pagan Gods of old. This reversion to pagan practices the Spaniards considered as witchcraft and must be dealt with summarily. A number of the Indian leaders were brought to trial; 43 were sentenced to be whipped and sold into slavery, 4 were to be hanged. However, on the concerted threat of several of the powerful pueblo leaders to use force, the governor, on payment of a tribute, found it expedient to release the imprisoned men. One of the men who was whipped, a Tewa tribal leader and native of San Juan pueblo, never forgot or forgave the indignity he suffered at the hands of the Spaniards. His name was Po-pé. (Po-PAY).

Po-pé, realizing the weakness of previous attempts of the Indians to throw off the yoke of Spanish control lay in the lack of a coordinated effort on the part of the many pueblos, sought to remedy this. Meetings of pueblo leaders were called, and secret and careful plans were worked out for a great and simultaneous rebellion in which every Indian village would join. Every Spaniard was to be destroyed, every vestige of the long period of foreign domination was to be wiped out. Especially were the forces of destruction to be focused on mission and convento to nullify completely the work of missionary and abolish the Christian faith. The ancient gods and ceremonies of the pueblos were to be restored.

On August 10, 1680 the fury of the Indians was let loose and vengeance ruled the countryside. Blood flowed freely that day of doom as unsuspecting padre and peaceful settler were struck down, many falling under blows from supposedly friendly Indian neighbors. The fathers died all sorts of deaths — some references say a resident priest was bound naked on a hog's back and paraded, beaten and killed by yelling mobs. Some Spaniards from nearby ranches managed to escape to Santa Fé, and with residents and officials of the city, sought shelter in the old Governor's Palace facing the plaza.

The triumphant rebels gathered in large numbers in the city, whooping, dancing, and raiding the homes of the Spaniards. The survivors, crowded in the *presidio,* now the Governor's Palace, were closely besieged, suffering great hardships. After several days the astute besiegers cut off the presidio water supply. Governor Antonio de Otermin and his officers then decided that the city must be abandoned. On August 21 the Spaniards, numbering a few more than 1,000, but still a formidable force, marched out from the citadel unmolested by the enemy. Traveling by the Galisteo Valley, women and children in the center, the expedition reached the friendly Indians of Isleta pueblo 70 miles south. It has been estimated that well over 1,000 colonists, 30 missionaries, and a number of devout Indians perished in the revolt.

With Isleta as a base, Governor Otermin made several sorties against the enemy only to find his reduced strength insufficient to make headway in regaining the province. It was therefore decided to continue the retreat to El Paso del Norte. Joined by some of the Isleta Indians, and gathering others as they passed through Socorro and San Antonio pueblos, the weary Spaniards began the long heartbreaking journey south. Through inhospitable country, over hazardous 90-mile *Jornada del Muerto* (Journey of Death) the weakened people struggled, to reach haven at last at Paso del Norte (present-day Ciudad Juárez) in Chihuahua, Mexico. Here across the river many of the colonists, and friendly Indians who retreated with them, made new homes.

In the north churches were burned, conventos destroyed, records, missals and documents were piled in the plazas and consumed in huge bonfires. Converted Indians were compelled to renounce their Christian beliefs, put through severe religious ceremonies as of old, and finally cleansed in baths of yucca suds. All Hispanic customs and the Spanish language were to be abolished under penalty of severe punishment. Most of the mission churches were so damaged that extensive rebuilding was necessary after the reconquest of 1692-93.

A few years after the rebellion a reaction set in among the pueblo people as they began to realize all that had been lost by the uprising. Life became less secure; harsh and unpleasant changes forced upon them by fanatical leaders interfered with their quiet daily life as practiced under the padres; and they were far from happy. Also the protection provided by the Spanish soldiers in restraining surrounding nomadic tribes from raiding crops and homes was removed. As a result there were a renewal of attacks by Navajos, Utes, Comanches and Apaches, all ancient enemies of the peaceful pueblos. Perhaps, thought the people, the Christian God and the strong arm of the Spaniards were not so bad after all: at least the soil could be tilled and families raised in safety.

In their zeal to abolish all traces of Spanish occupation the rebel Indian leaders forbade the use of fruits, vegetables and even the livestock introduced by the settlers. For years the pueblo people had become accustomed to a richer and more more varied diet aided by these introductions. To return to the more limited fare of corn, beans, and squash of earlier days was a real hardship. Dissatisfaction against the rebel leaders began to mount throughout the pueblos.

For twelve years the Indians held Santa Fé, occupied the Palace of the Governors, and appointed their own governor. The small corner chapel in the Palace was turned into a kiva and ancient ceremonies revived. Laws were made and edicts issued to all the people. In pre-Spanish times each pueblo had been a self-governing and independent community loyal only to its own elected leaders. Inevitable resistance to the new regime developed, and chaotic conditions prevailed.

In 1690 the Spanish authorities in Mexico, believing conditions were right, appointed Don Diego De Vargas as governor with orders to subdue the rebellious Indians. On August 21, 1692 De Vargas with 300 armed men, accompanied by a few missionaries, left El Paso del Norte. By rapid marches he reached Santa Fé September 13, and, making a peaceful entry, repossessed the city in the name of the king of Spain. With the old capital as headquarters his little army fanned out, and by the end of another year, by threat of force, or promise of amity, secured the surrender of most of the pueblos without bloodshed.

With the country subdued, De Vargas returned to Mexico to recruit additional soldiers and settlers. Returning to New Mexico, he brought with him 17 additional Franciscan missionaries to re-convert and re-build. New missions and villas with parish churches were to be erected. But some Pueblos rebelled again, and through 1696 DeVargas had to campaign to subjugate them. Indian population diminished greatly from war deaths, reprisal executions, enslavement, sickness, and exposure. Reinforcement by incoming Spanish settlers smothered effective Pueblo resistance after that date.

EL PASO DEL NORTE
Missions

arching north to New Mexico in 1598, the Don Juan de Oñate expedition reached the Rio Grande and encamped below the pass on the stream at a fording place. Early in May the expedition started for the pueblo country, crossed the river at the ford, and named it El Paso del Norte, a name perpetuated in the city of El Paso today. Oñate found numerous rancherias of the Mansos Indians in the vicinity of the river, a sedentary people who lived by tilling small plantations along the fertile banks.

During the 1600's with missionaries and colonists, soldiers and supply caravans passed between Mexico and the north, Paso del Norte developed into a small villa. Indians who lived nearby became familiar with the preaching of the long-gowned Franciscans and in time many became Christians. So many were converted that in 1630 their leaders requested a chapel be built for them and a resident priest appointed in charge.

For several years travelling friars preached to and cared for the converted Indians, and it was not until 1659 that a mission chapel was started at Paseo del Norte. On the 8th of December, feast day of Nuestra Señora de Guadalupe, the mission was started. A small adobe church and a small home for a padre were erected. The church, and its successor the mission church of today, were dedicated to the Virgin Mother

The much reconstructed old mission church at Juárez, Chih., across the river from El Paso, Tex.

Photo by El Paso Chamber of Commerce

of God, Nuestra Señora de Guadalupe. With a church and priest, more natives became converted to Christianity; before long the little chapel was too small and a larger church was planned.

It is the present mission church facing the old-time plaza in the city of Juárez that replaced the adobe building of 1659. The cornerstone of this building was blessed April 2, 1662; it was finished six years later. Its plan is that of a parallelogram with a long nave and recessed chancel. Topped with a flat earthern roof the chancel was lighted by a clerestory window. A semi-detached *campanario* or bell tower rises in three stages from a massive base. Two of the upper stages, graceful in design, are pierced with arched openings where hang the the mission bells; the third stage is a small dome upholding the Cross. Over the three centuries of its existence the old building has seen many changes. The interior has lost its early plainness and is richly embellished by gifts and offerings from the devout. Set back somewhat from the street, its ancient facade is overshadowed by the fine stone cathedral of the diocese of Ciudad Juárez.

Shortly after Mexico won her independence from Spain in 1821 she named the little settlement on the southwest bank of the Rio Grande Ciudad Juárez in honor of the Indian patriot Benito Pablo Juárez. When the war between the United States and Mexico was finished, the Rio Grande from a few miles above El Paso to the Gulf of Mexico became the international boundary. The small adobe village in Texas retained the name El Paso. Over the years the two border cities have prospered and live in neighborly amity today.

We have noted, after the 1680 rebellion of the pueblos in northern New Mexico, that several hundred Christian Indians accompanied the Spaniards in their retreat to Paso del Norte. These converted Indians and their padres founded small pueblos along the northeastern banks of the Rio Grande and built churches. With irrigation the land proved fertile and good crops were produced.

Nearest to El Paso is Ysleta, settled by Tigua Indians and named after their old home. The first church at Ysleta is thought to have been erected in 1682. Over the years the location of the mission was changed. Called the Mother Mission it has been rededicated many times. It is now administered by Jesuits who took control of the mission in 1881 and named it Our Lady of Carmel. Many of its parishioners are direct descendants of the Tigua Indians who so many years ago founded the little settlement, now part of greater El Paso.

Misión De La Purísima Concepcion Del Socorro not far from Ysleta, was founded by Piro Indians who formerly lived at Socorro on the Rio Grande. Joining with them in the retreat from the north were many Christian natives of the same language group, former residents of missions Abó, Quarai, Gran Quivira and the other Saline Pueblos deserted in the 1670's. From its first location the mission was removed to its present spot in 1683 after some of the Indians tried to kill their priest. The present building is an interesting example of a Spanish-American mission and replaces an earlier church washed away when the Rio Grande was in flood in 1829.

Presidio y Misión De San Elizario at San Elizario, Texas, was, as its name indicates, first constructed as a small Spanish garrison. The church had mission status, for many converted natives lived on rancherias in the vicinity. Later the mission was moved to its present location nearer Socorro. It is thought the church now stands very close to the original site of the first Oñate encampment in 1598.

These little Texas Rio Grande missions have suffered over the centuries from flood, fire, and, at times, neglect. Rebuilt, restored, and revered, the churches are now serving the Catholic population of nearby communities. Picturesque in the "mission" architectural tradition they are a valuable heritage from the past. Illustrations of the three El Paso churches may be seen on pages 108 and 109.

MISSIONS WEST OF ALBUQUERQUE

rom Albuquerque west U. S. High-66 traverses a region of sandy semi-desert, crosses an ancient lava flow of contorted black basalt, and emerges on the high piñon-clad plateau that forms the western section of New Mexico. In this high country in olden times were thought to lie the legendary pueblos of great wealth, the "Seven Cities of Cibola" so hopefully sought by Coronado and his men in 1540. It is really a region of startling scenic contrasts, framed by magnificent formations of brilliant red and yellow sandstone over which the ever-changing play of sun and shadow adds to the charm and mystery of the land. Between the distant cliffs and mesas narrow valleys reach back to lonely and remote canyons where thrive the native grasses.

Deep in the recesses of this legendary country Navajo families find water, build their earth-covered hogans, and, ranging their goats and sheep on the scanty vegetation, eke out a living. A patch of fertile soil produces corn, beans and squash which, supplemented by meat from the flock, comprise the daily fare. Near the hogan the women of the family may be combing or spinning wool from the sheep, or perhaps weaving the lovely and colorful rugs so desired by the discriminating purchaser. In the autumn the whole family gathers to harvest the delicious nut of the piñon pine, an outing which all enjoy and which provides a small cash income.

At 142 miles Highway 66 reaches Gallup, trading center for the vast Navajo Indian reservation. This small city is noted as the home of the annual Intertribal Indian Ceremonial. Held in August, it is a time when Ute, Apache, Navajo, Zuñi and Indians from far regions gather and participate in dances and ceremonies. Games, races and contests of all kinds take place; it is a time of great excitement for both visitors and Indians alike.

Fine exhibits of native craft work are to be seen in the large exhibition hall and connecting demonstration rooms. A wealth of originality evidences itself in the great variety of beautiful designs, in the skill of the artists, and in the clever use of native materials. Fine pottery, weaving and basketry — collectors' pieces all — illustrate generations of skill in the use of simple materials. Ornaments of silver, cast and tooled, some inlaid with turquoise, agate or jet, vie for the coveted blue ribbons of excellence.

Gallup is a convenient center from which one may easily reach many places of historic, archaeological, or scenic interest in western New Mexico and eastern Arizona.

Market scene as it could have appeared in the 17th century.

MISSION SAN JOSÉ
De La Laguna

 hortly after the reconquest of New Mexico by De Vargas in 1692 - 93, a number of Indians of different tribes, converted but homeless and wandering, their pueblos destroyed, presented a problem to the Spanish authorities. Searching for a place capable of supporting these farming people, Don Pedro Rodriguez Cubero, governor of the province, while journeying to Zuñi in 1699, set aside the present reservation at Laguna for them. Here a few years earlier many of the homeless people had gathered under the care of the Franciscan Antonio de Miranda and lived in peace. This land being unclaimed by other Indians, the governor allotted for the homeless people a large tract comprising some 125,000 acres. Water was available and good grazing abundant, which with fertile soil, enabled the industrious people to provide for their wants.

On a rocky ledge near a small lake — hence the name Laguna — stone and adobe homes were built. In time the little lake dried up, but springs were numerous, crops were good, and the pueblo increased in size and importance. A number of other plantations were established on the reservation where both water and good soil were found. The people were good farmers, progressive and adaptable. Over the years they assimilated with the white man's religion many of his

San José mission church was erected in 1699 in the pueblo of Laguna, which was founded by several remnant tribes after the Pueblo Rebellion of 1680–1692.

customs; at the same time a number of the age-old ceremonies have been retained.

By 1706 a mission had been established and a church erected, with a connecting convento. As missionaries at this time were not too plentiful in the province, for some years Laguna was administered from Ácoma. The fine church, dedicated to San José (Saint Joseph), is well over 250 years old and still serves the inhabitants of the pueblo.

The mission was built of stone laid up in adobe mortar. Constructed without transepts, it contains a long narrow nave, the upper end with angled walls forming the chancel or sanctuary. On the front a plain, stepped parapet, crowned with a large cross, rises above the great door. Rectangular openings high in the wall contain the two bells. One is very old and may have been brought from Acoma at the time of the founding of the mission; the other bears imprinted a starred-diamond cross and the date 1710. The church and convento, centered in the pueblo, with gleaming walls of white, stand well above the low brown homes of the Indians.

On entering the long (80 feet) nave, one is immediately aware of the small choir gallery overhead. Supported in front by a large crossbeam which in turn is carried on two supporting brackets, its nearness to the ceiling provides a vantage point from which the heavy weathered vigas and carved corbels can be studied. The ancient vigas give much character to the narrow interior, their long ranks broken only by a low clerestory window so placed as to admit daylight to reach the elaborately decorated chancel. The oldtime pulpit is still in place on the Epistle side of the nave.

A wealth of ornate design painted by native artists in brilliant hues adorns both walls and ceiling of the chancel of San José. Above the high altar a reredos covers the wall space. The lower section, divided into three sections by carved serpentine columns, frames in each panel a sacred painting. Above the panels a larger one contains a painting of three figures enclosed on either side by large S-scrolls. The side walls of the chancel are decorated with vertical panels of curvilinear designs that reach to the decorated ceiling. A unique representation of the heavenly bodies, the sun, moon and stars, framed in a richly decorated border covers the ceiling. On the nave walls above a plain dado are symbolic designs relating to the seasonal activities of tribal lore.

As one faces the church, to the left is the convento, a rambling structure of some 10 rooms arranged around an open patio. Covered walks surround the center of the patio where grew the favorite flowers and shrubs of the padres. This covered ambulatory provided easy ingress to the work rooms and living quarters of the priests.

As an integral part of every mission, classrooms were included in the convento. It was the duty of the missionary to teach his people how to pray, to conduct themselves during the services, and when able, to sing the chants.

Some of the young people were apt pupils and soon learned to play simple musical instruments. Color and harmonious sounds, both of which Indians were accustomed to using in their indigenous ceremonies, appealed to them and were no doubt a factor in helping the good padres in the work of conversion. Many of the missionaries, lonely in the daily round of duty, found relief in the teaching of music to the Indians. Music thus became an added attraction to the Christian service, a real joy to both instructor and his neophytes.

In common with all old mission structures where considerable adobe was used in the construction, San José Mission has required extensive rebuilding. According to old records, a great deal of work was done to the buildings in 1766. Again in more recent times the Committee for the Preservation and Restoration of New Mexican Mission Churches carried on much needed repairs. In 1936–37 the padre's home was remodeled and made more conformable to present day requirements.

ÁCOMA MISSION
and Pueblo

ome 5 miles west of Albuquerque and 16 miles south of Highway 66 is situated the age-old home of the Ácoma Indians. As the winding road enters the reservation two high buff-colored buttes of sandstone are seen rising abruptly from the sandy plain. First encountered is the Enchanted Mesa, called by the Spaniards *Mesa Encantada*, a great rock, precipitous and inaccessible, rising a massive 430 feet above the level plain.

In the dim past, according to legends of the Ácomas, the flat summit of this great rock was once the home of some of their people. One day in summer — so the story goes — while most of the inhabitants were tilling their crops on the plain below, a terrible storm broke over the summit of the mesa and the only path to the village was shattered by a blast of lightning. It was, presumably, a crude rock stairway hacked out between a split section of the cliff and the more solid rock wall. With the only means of reaching the desert below destroyed, the unfortunate ones who had remained in the pueblo perished of starvation. Climbers reaching the summit in the early 1900's found only scant evidence of human occupation to substantiate the old legend.

Present-day Ácoma is built on the 70-acre summit of the larger mesa. This imposing block of sandstone, 357 feet high, has been the home of the Indians for a period long pre-dating the coming of the Spanish in 1540. It is still a veritable "City

Largest of the early mission churches of the Southwest is Ácoma, at the skytop pueblo of the same name.

Photo by New Mexico State Tourist Bureau

in the Sky", fascinating, picturesque, and extremely interesting. From a distance the cube-like rows of dwellings appear to be part of the natural rock, for, constructed of native stone, the horizontal lines of the houses blend with the sharply planed lines of the summit ledges. Above the pueblo dwellings rises the old mission church dominated by its twin bell towers.

Parking the car at the base of the cliff, one climbs a long incline of drifted sand which leads to the summit pueblo. A few stone steps complete the path, which ends immediately behind the rear of the great stone church. To the right the convento walls still stand, weathered reminders of the days when a resident padre lived on the rock.

From these high ledges superb views in all directions reward the visitor for his climb. Distant red and purple mountains ring the horizon; fantastic in shape and outline, mysterious and far-reaching, they form a brilliant and theatrical background for the vast plains below. A few ponies, dwarfed by the height, graze upon the scanty grasses of the desert. Indeed, gazing at the widespread scene, one feels that here is a landscape in which time has wrought little change. As the pueblo appears today — except for the church and a few new dwellings — so it must have looked to Don Hernando de Alvarado, first of the Spaniards to visit it some 420 years ago

The houses, built in long rows with passages or "streets" between, are terraced two and three stories high. In early days all lower rooms were entered through a hatch in the roof. Today these are storage rooms; the upper rooms reached by leaning ladders are the living quarters. Conveniently placed among the dwellings are numerous beehive-shaped adobe ovens where the Indian women do their baking. These are not an Indian invention, but were introduced by Spaniards.

Ácoma mission, dedicated to San Estéban Rey (Saint Stephen) is assumed to date from 1629, the church being erected between that date and 1641, during the period when Fray Juan Ramirez was the first resident missionary in the pueblo. As in other Indian pueblos, it is probable that services were first held in a rented room, perhaps later in a small chapel which may have stood close to the site of the present church. In recent years, at old mission sites, foundations of early chapels have been uncovered, a clear indication that smaller chapels usually preceded the erection of the larger mission churches.

It has been claimed the first large church built at Ácoma was destroyed during the Rebellion of 1680. We may doubt this, because records of damage to mission buildings at that time seldom tell of the complete razing of large structures stone by stone. The present church may therefore contain portions of the walls of the 1629 building. Today this fine old structure is one of the most attractive of the early surviving Franciscan Mission churches in New Mexico.

San Estéban Rey is indeed a splendid example of early stone and adobe construction. Measuring 150 feet long, 40 feet wide, and with walls 60 feet high and 10 feet thick, it is truly a noble building to be perched upon a rocky mesa 350 feet above the desert floor. Heavy pine vigas carry the high roof; 50 feet long and hewn 14 inches square (some have been replaced with round timbers) they were cut in mountain forests 30 miles to the south. Transported on the shoulders of the devout — according to tradition — they were wrestled up the steep cliff with great labor. Looking at the front elevation of the noble building one notes that the sturdiness of the structure is emphasized by two buttress-like square towers. In them open belfries display the ancient bells suspended from weathered timbers.

An old cemetery (Campo Santo) fronting the church is unique testimonial to the devotion of the people to their religion. High retaining walls were constructed, enclosing an area perhaps 200 feet square. This was filled with earth laboriously carried up in baskets from the plain below by the women of the tribe, to the end that their dead might rest in consecrated ground.

Stepping through the great door into the quiet interior of

the church, one finds the air is refreshingly cool, for thick stone and adobe walls shut out the summer heat. As the building is without transepts or a clerestory window the interior is but dimly lighted by the choir-gallery window and two others high in the east wall. The long rectangular nave, with hard-packed earthen floor and time-stained walls, is indeed a comfortless and primitive place of worship with only the Stations of the Cross to relieve the plainness of the walls.

The end wall of the chancel contains a richly painted reredos completely filling the space from high altar to ceiling. It is divided into nine panels by ornately carved columns, serpentine in form, each of which frames a primitive oil painting of a saint. A few other old paintings adorn the church walls, among them the one of Saint Joseph which is noteworthy both for its historic interest and its extensive travels. First brought to Ácoma by the Franciscan Juan Ramirez in 1629, the painting is assumed to have been given personally to the priest by King Charles II of Spain. To the devout inhabitants of the pueblo, and also those of nearby Laguna pueblo (who once claimed the painting) the picture is believed to possess miraculous powers. It is still greatly venerated by the Indians today.

In the old days a comfortable convento home of the padre was attached to the right side of the church and was so constructed that it overlooked the pueblo. Most of the walls of this ancient building are still standing, showing that the rooms once enclosed a small, secluded patio. Wind-blown sands have buried the onetime patio garden which in its day must have been a veritable oasis, green with fruit trees, vines, vegetables, and flowers to grace the padre's table.

On the pueblo side of the convento second-story rooms connected with a small loggia or roofed veranda. Here the padre lived and took his ease behind the now sand-blasted railing; here he could admire the distant view and at the same time keep a watchful eye on his flock. The lower rooms of the convento housed his servants and also served as classrooms for the instruction of young Indians.

In Willa Cather's historical novel of southwestern mission life, "Death Comes to the Archbishop", she includes an episode of mission life at Ácoma.

Of all the Indian pueblos which resisted the Spaniards in 1540 and during the bloody 1600's, Ácoma, the "Sky City" of the conquistadors, suffered the least damage to its sturdy rock-walled homes. Planted firmly upon its sandstone foundation, the dwellings in this ancient pueblo today serve as homes for only a portion of the tribe, for the majority of the people have scattered, now that the Navajos no longer raid, to the farming villages closer to their widespread fields, returning to the venerated mesatop pueblo only for the age-old ceremonies.

Each year its sons and daughters gather around the old mission church on the feast day of Saint Stephen, celebrating first the Mass, then the traditional dances and tribal ceremonies of the pueblo, to be followed by a real Old Home Day.

Truly a visit to Ácoma and its Franciscan church, perhaps the oldest continuously occupied community on the North American continent, is an unforgettable experience in these restless days.

ZUÑI PUEBLO
and Mission

 pproximately 35 miles south of Gallup lies the reservation and large pueblo of the Zuñi Indians. Surrounded by pine-clad mountains and nestled in the shadow of great Towayalone (Mountain of the Sacred Corn), the village occupies part of the site of ancient Halona, one of the six Zuñi pueblos of Coronado's time.

Abandoned since 1846, the Zuñi mission church looked like this before restoration work began in 1966. The 17th-century church was larger.

Photo by New Mexico State Tourist Bureau

Approaching the pueblo from the east we see, in the distance, blue smoke of piñon and juniper wood rising from many small fires in the red stone houses. Cube-like blocks of homes (a few terraced), irregular in outline, open on small courts where busy women carry on the daily tasks, interrupted perhaps by laughing children, or an inquisitive burro or two. Weathered ladders of wood reach to upper floors where other housewives are busy on the roofs.

Here and there throughout the pueblo are larger courts or plazas, settings for the frequent ceremonial dances, at which time the whole village takes on a festive air. Best known of the old dances and the one attracting the most visitors is the colorful Shalako. During this ceremony, performed late in the year, the impersonators of the Gods appear, bless new homes, and give thanks for the abundant harvest of field and flock. The ancient, fertile plantations of the pueblo bordering the Zuñi River provide ample crops and good range land for the people.

Rising high among the terraced homes on the south side

of the pueblo is the crumbling ruin of the old Franciscan church of Halona, Mission Señora de Guadalupe. One of three early churches erected for the Zuñi people, it is believed to date from the year 1639. It was partially destroyed when Navajos raided the pueblo in 1673. Fire consumed the timbers but much of the thick adobe walls remained standing. The mission is assumed to have been rebuilt in 1706.

Hawikuh, 14 miles from the modern pueblo, first seen by the conquistadors four centuries ago, was at that time the largest of the six Zuñi pueblos. A greatly exaggerated description of this village as given by Fray Marcos de Niza added strength to the legend of the treasure-rich "Seven Cities of Cibola." On the occasion of the visit of Juan de Oñate in 1593 to the Zuñis only six of the pueblos were occupied. Today rock-strewn ruins mark the sites of most of the early villages.

Three missionaries were sent to Hawikuh early in the 1600's, the first services being held in the plaza upon a plat-

Zuñi mission church as excavated, stabilized, and restored under technical supervision by the National Park Service with funds provided by the Catholic church.

Photo by New Mexico State Tourist Bureau

form. Later the missionaries purchased a house in the pueblo, using it both as a home and chapel until a mission could be erected. Old documents indicate three churches were established for the Zuñi people by 1629: one at Hawikuh, one at Kechipayan, and the third at Halona.

The work of the Franciscans at Zuñi was not very successful; differences soon appeared, friction developed, and as early as 1632 two of the missionaries were killed. Again in the Rebellion of 1680 Father Juan de Val perished and the churches were despoiled.

After the Rebellion, the people, fearing reprisals, abandoned their scattered villages and erected new homes on the summit of Towayalone where they remained for several years. With a promise of peace, after the reconquest by De Vargas, the people left their windswept aerie and returned to Halona where they built new homes.

Franciscans were again assigned to the Zuñi Indians and a church and convento — the present ruin — reconstructed in 1706 in the center of the pueblo. Trouble soon developed between the domineering padres and the village leaders and it was necessary to station a small garrison of Spanish soldiers in the pueblo. Early in the 1800's weakness in the civil situation in Santa Fé compelled the withdrawal of the garrison, after which the Zuñi people lost no time in expelling the unwanted missionaries. From that time on the Spaniards lost interest in attempting to convert the Zuñis.

Mission Nuestra Señora de Guadalupe, the old ruin in the pueblo, is not hard to find as one threads the narrow lanes south of the Zuñi Post Office. The church, all that remains of the mission, is now a forlorn picture of a once fine building, a ruin rapidly filling with wind-blown sand, crumbling adobe and fallen timbers. The marked neglect of the ancient church reveals strongly the lingering resentment of the Indians to long years of unwilling submission to the Spanish padres.

In its prime the church was a fine example of Spanish-Indian mission architecture of the early 1700's. Its long nave (about 80 feet) and small sanctuary, its flat roof carried on 36 hewn vigas, the choir gallery over the main entrance, all conformed to the plan of early churches. Although the floor was of hard-packed adobe, the interior must have been quite attractive. Traces of carving on carrying beams, and other features, indicate the interior to have been nicely finished. A clerestory window provided light to the chancel.

———————⋖◉⋗———————

So wrote Author Parsons in 1965, but in 1966 the Catholic church and the Zuñi tribe furnished funds for the National Park Service to supervise an historically accurate restoration of the church. An interesting innovation was the use of a hand-operated hydraulic press, which turned out adobe bricks four per minute, ready for use, eliminating sun drying.

The Zuñis, industrious farmers and for centuries the premier lapidaries of the Southwest, produce beautiful silver jewelry, and work in shell, jet, coral and turquoise. They are insisting on an increasing share of independence in conducting their tribal affairs.

HOPI MISSIONS

arthest west of all the pueblo-dwelling people, the Hopi, or Moqui (mo-kee) Indians as they were called by the Spaniards, then, as now, live in the land of desert mesas that lie on the plateau of northeastern Arizona, the Painted Desert country.

In 1540 while Coronado was recuperating from wounds received in the attack on Hawikuh, rumors reached him of people to the north who lived in stone villages on high table mountains. To keep his restless men busy exploring he

sent a small party under the leadership of Don Pedro de Továr to investigate the rumored pueblos. It is thought that the first Hopi pueblo to be visited by Továr was Awatovi. The Indians, who were aware of the attack by the Spaniards on Hawikuh, were reluctant to meet the white men and Továr had to use force against them. He found the Hopis to be farming people, living in crudely constructed homes of stone on cliff-like mesas that rose abruptly from the sandy plain. Possessing neither mineral wealth nor other riches, the inhabitants wrested a meager living from small farm plots watered by clever use of the scant supply. From the Indians Továr learned of a great river far to the north, a rumor that Coronado thought should be investigated.

Coronado immediately dispatched a party of 25 horsemen under the command of Don Garcia López de Cárdenas to search for the rumored river. Receiving directions from the Hopis they proceeded north for 20 days to arrive finally at the brink of the canyon. To Cárdenas and his men, therefore, goes the credit of being the first white men to gaze upon the marvelous and colorful Grand Canyon of the Colorado River.

When Don Juan de Oñate founded his first settlement in the Rio Grande valley in 1598, he promptly assigned his missionaries to the fields in which they were to labor at the great task of converting the native peoples. Father Andrés Corchado was given jurisdiction over the Indians of Ácoma, Zuñi and Hopi. To cover this vast territory in those early days was an impossible task and nothing was accomplished: in fact Father Corchado is believed to have returned to Mexico in 1601.

During the next 25 years the small number of missionaries in the province was fully occupied in working in the many pueblos along the Rio Grande. Even when the friars were backed by the military and civil authorities, the work was discouragingly slow because many Indians were extremely reluctant to forsake aboriginal beliefs.

In 1629, 30 additional Franciscans arrived from Mexico, thereby enabling the assignment of missionaries to more dis-

Awatobi mission church as it may have looked. Based on excavated foundations. Bell towers were round, however. 91
Reconstruction by Harold A. Wolfinbarger, Jr.

tant pueblos. Devoted men journeyed to the Saline Pueblos to the east, while others followed long and dangerous trails west to the home of the Ácoma, Zuñi and Hopi peoples.

Two fathers, Francisco Porras and Andres Gutierrez, and a lay brother were sent to work among the Hopis, reaching Awatovi pueblo on the 20th of August 1629, feast day of Saint Bernard. It soon seemed to these men that the friendly people would be receptive to their teachings and the pueblo a likely place at which to found a mission. A mission here could well be a center from which, in time, the other Hopi villages would come under its influence.

Before long, with Indian help, the walls of a large church and convento began to rise, a most ambitious project which the fathers dedicated as Misión San Bernardo de Aquátibi, thus honoring the saint's day of their arrival. In later years the Franciscans founded several other small missions on the Hopi mesas.

During the great Pueblo Rebellion of 1680 the fine church at Awatovi suffered destruction, but the convento was spared. In fact, after the expulsion of the Spaniards, many Hopis took possession of the well-built convento quarters, dividing the larger rooms into smaller ones, thus converting the building into an Indian pueblo.

Our interest is centered in the old church of Misión San Bernardo, long buried under the drifting sands of the desert. Constructed with stone and adobe, its plan was functional, conforming to the traditional design of early Franciscan pueblo churches in the province. Although the plan was simple, the conception of both church and convento was ambitious, the decorations elaborate.

A high and imposing front (postulated) faced to the east, flanked at each corner by a round bell tower. Flanking the base of each tower was a small square room, the room to the left being the baptistry (a foundation for a central font and the the customary corner drain indicated its use). The room on the right would appear to have been the porter's lodge or waiting room. Between the tower foundations were evidences of posts; it is assumed these supported a small exterior balcony over the great doors, spanning the space between the two towers. This was an architectural feature often found in the older churches of the Southwest.

The nave of San Bernardo, long and narrow, was constructed without transepts, its hard-packed floor of adobe still firm and smooth when uncovered. The narrow west end of the church forming the chancel contained space for three altars. During daytime services the chancel would be flooded with light shining through a transverse clerestory window at the upper end of the nave. Only two doorways were found giving entrance to the church proper: one of course was the imposing front entrance where swung heavy double doors of paneled wood. The back stile of large church doors at that time was usually rounded at both ends to form pivots; embedded in the masonry of the door frame these pivots made efficient hinges upon which the door would swing. A small door in the right wall of the chancel provided convenient access to the padre's private chapel, and to rooms in the convento.

Whenever possible the Franciscans embellished and enriched their churches and conventos by using color, by carving and decorating the plain woodwork, and by displaying such attractive altar linens and furnishings as they possessed. Brilliant murals, sometimes done by the friars themselves, and sometimes by native artists under their direction, often covered the chancel walls, the lower section of the nave, the baptistry, and other chambers. Even the common and classrooms in the convento were brightened where possible. The missionaries knew by experience that a richly decorated house of worship added to the feeling of awe and reverence on the part of aboriginal worshippers. The Indians have always been responsive to color, surrounded as they are with the brilliancy of their native land: even in aboriginal kivas color and wall decoration played an important part in the ancient ceremonies. The clever missionary appreciated the love of color on the part of his people as well as their skill in the use of local materials, and put this ability to work in building and glorifying his churches.

When Mission San Bernardo was excavated by archaeologists in the late 1930's many fragmants of painted plaster were found in the debris. Executed in earthen colors of brilliant hue were crude copies of the glazed tiles that are such an attractive feature of all ecclesiastical buildings in both Spain and Mexico. Repeated layers of color on some of the plaster fragments proved these decorations to have been frequently renewed.

In the debris on the chancel floor a small piece of a richly painted border came to light. From its position it is believed to have been part of the facing decoration of the high altar. Colored plaster, too was found on a portion of the lower wall of the nave, indicating a painted dado such as found in mission churches today.

After securing the submission of the Rio Grande pueblos in 1692-93 De Vargas set out for Hopiland to effect the re-consecration of the people and reactivation of the missions there. Since some success had been attained, Father Juan de Garaycoechea, who in 1699 reopened the Zuñi mission at Halona, proceeded the next year to Awatovi and found the neophyte Indians had repaired a section of Mission San Bernardo, converting three large rooms in the convento into a chapel. These Christianized people were truly glad to have again a resident padre living in the pueblo.

Resentment in the other Hopi pueblos at the return of the missionaries was very strong, and constant pressure was exerted on the people of Awatovi to make them abandon the Christian religion. Stress increased, and in 1701 when the padre was visiting in Zuñi the non-Christian Indians attacked the pueblo, massacred most of the converts and sacked the mission. After this awful demonstration of hostility all missionary activity concerning the Hopis ceased and Misión San

Bernardo de Awátovi became a ruin shunned by all, the pueblo deserted.

The importance the Franciscans attached to the Hopi country, their wish to make of Awatovi an important Christian center, is emphasized by the discoveries made by archaeologists in the 1930's. To the right of San Bernardo church a foundation of a much larger church came to light. Cruciform in shape, its walls about 6 feet thick, this was intended to be a massive and important building indeed. There was however no evidence that more than the foundation was ever constructed. Also, a little distant, other foundations were found. These have been studied carefully and reveal that a large stable with stalls for 12 horses, storage rooms, and space for a garrison had been planned. This building also was never finished. The two foundations clearly show the importance the Franciscan friars attached to the pueblo of Awatovi as headquarters for Christian endeavor.

For the fascinating story of this frontier mission we have to thank the careful archaeologists, who in 1935–39, under the auspices of the Peabody Museum of Cambridge, Mass., excavated the ruins. The results of this work including the skillful conjectural reconstruction of the buildings by Ross Gordon Montgomery, Watson Smith, John Otis Brew, and others have revealed to us a picture of this distant outpost of the Spanish program to Christianize the natives of the then province of western New Mexico.

The ruins of Misión San Bernardo de Awátovi are again vanishing beneath the drifting sands of the desert. They can be reached from Keams Canyon in the Hopi Reservation.

To visit Awatovi, you should obtain permission from the Hopis, who understandably have become irked by litter and vandalism.

THE MISSION
SUPPLY SERVICE

e must tell here the story of the vital supply service carried on from Mexico to the northern province — a service without which both mission endeavor and Spanish settlements would perish. An understanding of the many great problems met and overcome in those early days of difficult traveling is needed to appraise properly the fine work of the Franciscans in the founding of their great missions in New Mexico.

In the early 16th century when Spain embarked on its great era of discovery and exploration each expedition had its quota of religious leaders, members of monastic orders devoted to the spreading of the Christian faith among the heathen. In the search for new lands to conquer, new wealth to gain, and favorable sites in which to plant colonies, missionaries played an important part. Close to the heart of the royal house of Spain was the determination that all conquered peoples should eventually be brought into the Christian fold.

At all times large sums of money were required properly to equip and maintain a major expedition. Ships, men and vast quantities of supplies were needed. Funds largely were furnished by the leaders themselves or their wealthy friends or patrons. The Crown encouraged the adventurers, participated in the expenses to a limited degree, and received a percentage of the spoils which was allotted to the royal treasury.

On the journey and in the field Masses were said every morning and before battle. This gave courage to the soldiers, who, convinced that they were instruments of the Lord in bringing light to the heathen, fought with great determination. Aided by superior arms (and Indian allies) they were enabled to prevail over large numbers of natives who with cruder weapons tried to defend their homes. Thus it was in Mexico, in Peru, in central America. and in the valley of the Rio Grande to the north.

With the entradas of Coronado, Espejo, Oñate, and others to the pueblo country it was members of the Franciscan Order Minor, men who specialized in missionary work, who accompanied them. It was to be their task to guide the Indians, by example and teaching, into the path of the True Faith. In later years, when many new missions were being founded, the Crown assumed the expenses incurred by the religious. Only in this way could the royal house be sure the work of conversion would continue without interruption. As settlements and missions increased in number, friction developed between religious leaders and military authorities; the constant support by Spain and Mexico was therefore necessary if further expansion of mission work was to continue. For well over 200 years disciples of Saint Francis of Assisi carried on the intensive and exacting work of converting the Indians of New Mexico.

In early days traveling missionaries carried portable altars, each equipped with four stout staffs to support an awning. The altar could be quickly set up in field or village, vestments donned by the priest, and services held. To the natives the field equipment of the friars was an object of considerable interest. They noted the reverence paid by commander and rough soldier to the observance of the Mass. It was natural for them to wonder about the white man's medicine, a magic that so strangely subdued and affected its followers. In many cases they were ready to listen to the lay brother interpreter of the missionary.

We have seen how, at the time of the first permanent settlements in the province, missionaries were assigned areas, in the pueblos of which they were to teach the Indians the Christian message. Singly or in pairs they walked the narrow village lanes, set up their little altars in the central plazas, and through interpreters sought to influence the people. In time, as some of the pueblos proved amenable, small chapels were built. The padres, being men of learning, soon mastered the Indian languages and so were able to reach greater numbers of the inhabitants. All progress was reported to the Franciscan commissary-general in Mexico City, and in 1609, everything appearing favorable for the spread of Christianity, the Crown assumed the total cost of mission work in the province. For the missions, both old and those projected, a regular supply service from Mexico was inaugurated under the control of the official procurator of custody. By 1631 the number of missionaries serving in the northern province had been stabilized at 66, this number remaining constant until the pueblo uprising of 1680.

Every three years mission caravans of heavy vehicles, loaded with supplies for the religious, set out from Mexico City. Hub deep in sand, over long stretches of arid desert and windswept upland, the caravans moved steadily north on the perilous journey of some 1700 miles to the capital at Santa Fé. These triennial supply trains, so essential to maintain existing missions and for the founding of new, like the mail of today, always got through.

Each caravan consisted of 33 *carros* (wagons), one being allotted for each two friars serving in the colony. As the Franciscan commissary-general in Mexico City was solicitous that new missions be established as rapidly as possible, considerable space in the wagons was devoted to articles essential for their founding and construction. The balance of the cargo space was filled with the necessary replenishment of supplies to maintain existing missions, and with clothing and other per-

A caravan of "carros" (wagons) on the trail with supplies for the frontier missions.
Drawing by Harold A. Wolfinbarger, Jr.

sonal articles for the friars. For each new mission with its projected church and convento careful attention was given to its requirements. Only those articles or materials unobtainable in the colony — and they were legion — could occupy the precious space.

We have shown how mission buildings, church and convento, were constructed with available native materials, of stone or adobe. Even then certain essentials must be imported if the missions are properly to be fitted out and greater churches are to grace the land. Tools and a multitude of other things must come from the older colony.

Stone or adobe walls can be constructed with the primitive tools of the natives, but for the massive vigas metal axes, saws, adzes, augurs and planes were required to shape the heavy timbers. Doors, closets, and the simple furniture for the convento required nails, latches and hinges, none of which could be produced in New Mexico during its infancy. To furnish properly the church itself, sacred vessels, fine fabrics, a large and small bell, a painting or two for the chancel, wax for candles, incense for the censer, and missals for the Mass and music were musts.

To replace the depleted stores of existing missions, sacramental wine—perhaps in later days made in the colony—beeswax, sackcloth for new robes, linen, sandals and a multitude of lesser articles that could only come from Mexico or the mother country were included.

Starting in a simple way the service soon became organized but lacked a regular schedule. During the great period of mission expansion, or between the years 1627 to 1655, one Tomás Manso (later Bishop Manso) was appointed procurator-general for the New Mexico missions. Under his able direction the triennial caravan service became properly organized and its regularity assured. The dependable service rendered by the caravans gave confidence to the Franciscans and enabled the work of expansion and conversion to flourish.

GLOSSARY

Ácoma	AH-ko-mah	Jornada del Muerto	hor-NAH-dah dell moo-AIR-toh
Albuquerque	al-bu-KUR-kee		
Awátobi	a-WAH-toh-bee	Jumanas	hoo-MAH-nahs
Benevides	bay-nah-VEE-dace	*kiva*	KEE-vah
		Laguna	lah-GOO-nah
Comanche	koh-MAHN-chee	*mesa*	MAY-sah
Campo Santo	KAHM-poh SAHN-to	Oñate	own-YAH-tay
		Pecos	PAY-kohs
Chamuscado	chah-mus-KAH-do	Piro	PEE-roh
		plazuela	plah-ZWAY-lah
Cíbola	SEE-bo-lah	Puaray	POOH-are-eye
conquistadores	kohn-kees-tah-DOH-race	Quarai	QUAR-eye
despoblado	dace-poh-BLAH-do	Ramirez	rah-MEE-race
		Rodriguez	roh-DREE-gays
entrada	ehn-TRAH-dah	Tano	TAH-noh
Espejo	ace-PAY-hoh	Taos	rhymes with house
San Felipe	sahn fay-LEE-pay		
		Tewa	TAY-wah
Galisteo	gah-lees-TAY-oh	Tiguex	TEE-guesh
Gran Quivira	grahn kee-VEE-rah	Tiwa	TEE-wah
		Towayalone	toh-wah-YAH-lo-nay
Hopi	HOH-pee		
Hawiku	HAH-wee-kuh	*villa*	VEEL-yah
Isidro	ee-SEE-droh	*vega*	VAY-gah
Isleta	ee-SLAY-tah	*viga*	VEE-gah
Jemez	HAY-mess	Zia	SEE-yah
Juan	huan or whahn	Zuñi	ZOON-yee

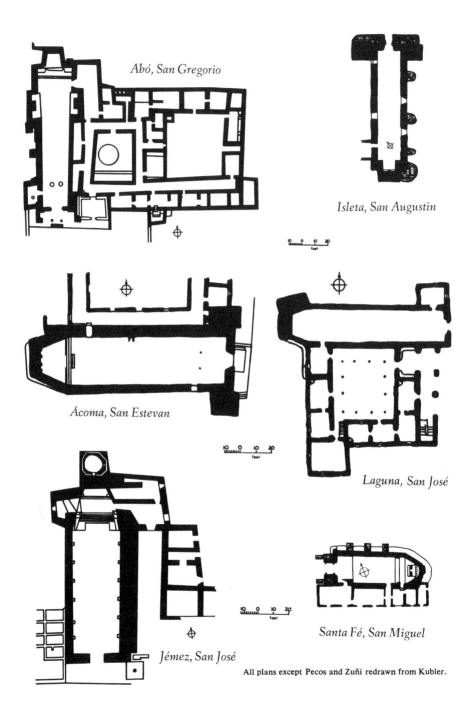

Abó, San Gregorio

Isleta, San Augustin

Ácoma, San Estevan

Laguna, San José

Jémez, San José

Santa Fé, San Miguel

All plans except Pecos and Zuñi redrawn from Kubler.

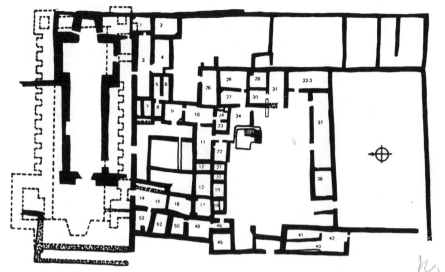

Pecos, Nuestra Señora de los Angeles de Porciúncula. The under-lying 17th-century church is in dotted outline.

Quarai, La Concepcion

Zuñi, Nuestra Señora de Guadalupe

Socorro, San Miguel

Ysleta church (above), oldest building in Texas, was founded in 1682 by refugee Tigua Indians. Is much remodeled, but still in daily use.

Photo by El Paso Chamber of Commerce

Socorro church (opposite page) was founded in the early 1770's.

Photo by El Paso Chamber of Commerce

San Elizario church (below), "youngest of El Paso's trio of old churches was founded in 1777 as a military chapel for use of the Spanish soldiers.

Photo by El Paso Chamber of Commerce

SUGGESTED READING

Bolton, Herbert E.

1916. Edtr. *Spanish Exploration in the Southwest, 1542-1706*. Barnes and Noble, New York:.

1949. *Coronado, Knight of Pueblos and Plains*. Univ. of New Mexico Press, Albuquerque, N.M.

Dominguez, Fray Francisco, tsltd. by Eleanor Adams and Fray Angélico Chavez

1956. *The Missions of New Mexico, 1776*. Univ. of New Mexico Press, Albuquerque, N.M.

Dutton, Bertha P.

1952. Highlights of the Jemez Region, *El Palacio*, Vol. 59, No. 5, Museum of New Mexico, Santa Fé, N.M.

Hammond, George P.

1926-7. Don Juan de Oñate and the Founding of New Mexico, *Publications in History*, Vol. 2, *Historical Society of New Mexico*. Santa Fé, N.M.

Hayes, Alden C.

1974. *The Four Churches of Pecos*. Univ. of New Mexico Press, Albuquerque, N.M.

Hewett, Edgar L., and Fisher, Reginald

1943. *Mission Monuments of New Mexico*. Univ. of New Mexico Press, Albuquerque, N.M.

Kidder, Alfred V.

1951. The Story of the Pueblo of Pecos, *El Palacio*, Vol. 58, No. 3, Museum of New Mexico, Santa Fé, N.M.

Kubler, George

1940. *The Religious Architecture of New Mexico*. The Taylor Museum, Colorado Springs, Colo.

Lummis, C. F.

1913. *The Land of Poco Tiempo*. Chas. Scribner's Sons, New York.

Montgomery, Ross Gordon, Watson Smith and John Otis Brew
1949. *Franciscan Awatovi*. *Peabody Museum Papers*, Vol. XXXVI, Report No. 3. Published by the Museum at Cambridge, Mass.

Regan, A. B.
1914. *Don Diego, or the Pueblo Uprising in 1680*. George Parker, translator and Editor. New York.

Scholes, France V.
1930. The Supply Service of the New Mexico Missions in the 17th Century, *New Mexico Historical Review*, Vol. 5.
1937. Church and State in New Mexico, 1610-1650, *New Mexico Historical Society, Publications in History*, Vol. 7, June.

Sinclair, John L.
1951. The Story of the Pueblo of Kuaua, *El Palacio*, Vol. 58, No. 7. Museum of New Mexico, Santa Fé, N.M.

Smith, Watson
1970. Seventeenth-Century Spanish Missions of the Western Pueblo Area. *The Smoke Signal*, No. 21, Tucson Corral of the Westerners, Tucson, Arizona.

Stubbs, Stanley A.
1959. "New" Old Churches Found at Quarai and Tabirá (Pueblo Blanco), *El Palacio*, Vol. 66, No. 5, Museum of New Mexico, Santa Fé, N.M.

Toulouse, Joseph H., Jr.
1938. The Mission of San Gregorio de Abó, *El Palacio*, Vol. 45, No. 24. Museum of New Mexico, Santa Fé, N.M.
1940. San Gregorio de Abó Mission, *El Palacio*, Vol. 47, No. 3. Museum of New Mexico, Santa Fé, N.M.

Winship, George Parker
1896. The Coronado Expedition, 1540-1642, *Bureau of American Ethnology, Annual Report* No. 14, Smithsonian Institution, Washington, D.C.

INDEX